School is Sacred

Music and Spirituality

Series Editor
June Boyce-Tillman

Vol. 17

School is Sacred

A Philosophy of Education for Our Time

Iris M. Yob

PETER LANG

Oxford · Berlin · Bruxelles · Chennai · Lausanne · New York

Bibliographic Information published by the Deutsche Nationalbibliothek
The Deutsche Nationalbibliothek lists this publication in the Deutsche Nationalbibliografie; detailed bibliographic data is available online at http://dnb.d-nb.de.

Library of Congress Cataloging-in-Publication Data
Names: Yob, Iris M., author.
Title: School is Sacred: A Philosophy of Education for Our Time / Iris M. Yob.
Description: Oxford; New York: Peter Lang, [2026] | Series: Music and spirituality, 2296-164X; volume 17 | Includes bibliographical references and index.
Identifiers: LCCN 2024060180 (print) | LCCN 2024060181 (ebook) | ISBN 9781803746852 (paperback) | ISBN 9781803746869 (ebook) | ISBN 9781803746876 (epub)
Subjects: LCSH: Education--Philosophy. | Education--Social aspects. | Schools.
Classification: LCC LB14.7 .Y63 2025 (print) | LCC LB14.7 (ebook) | DDC 370.1--dc23/eng/20250117
LC record available at https://lccn.loc.gov/2024060180
LC ebook record available at https://lccn.loc.gov/2024060181

ISSN 2296-164X
ISBN 978-1-80374-685-2 (Print)
ISBN 978-1-80374-686-9 (E-PDF)
ISBN 978-1-80374-687-6 (E-PUB)
DOI 10.3726/b22204

Published by Peter Lang Ltd, Oxford (United Kingdom)

info@peterlang.com

This publication has been peer reviewed.

www.peterlang.com

The essence of education is that it be religious.
Pray, what is religious education?
A religious education is one which inculcates duty and reverence.
And the foundation of reverence is this perception, that the present
holds within itself the complete sum of existence,
backwards and forwards,
that whole amplitude of time,
which is eternity.

Alfred North Whitehead, *The Aims of Education* (1929)

Table of Contents

CHAPTER 1

Setting the Stage

The award-winning movie, *Lunana: A Yak in the Classroom*, is a fictional account of an indifferent teacher who must fulfill his five-year contract in government service. He is appointed against his wishes to a teaching post in Lunana, the most remote school in Bhutan, and probably the most remote school in the world. The emphasis of the Bhutanese government, reflecting the slogan Gross National Happiness, is seen in part to depend on education for all, making the schools a focus of effort for the country. In Lunana, reflecting the reality of life lived on the edge where having a teacher is not always possible, the people have a deep devotion and veneration for the school and its teacher. The whole community travels miles to meet the new teacher as he is forced to trek for days into this remote village. They proudly show him the school, so poor, that precious paper is taped to the windows to keep the cold out and no books or teaching aids can be found within. The classroom is covered in dust from disuse. But the villagers enfold this reluctant teacher into their community so much so that he can never forget them or the bright faces of his students or the value of his simple instruction to these children of yak herders.

In one early scene that begins to point the teacher to the greater reality of what he is called to be and do as a teacher, a young local leader shows him how to light his fire with yak dung. The city-bred teacher exclaims,

> *"You are too respectful. My friends would think it was so funny."*
> *"Well, you are a teacher."*
> *"A teacher is just like everybody else."*
> *"A teacher guides our children to follow the right path."*
> *"The right path?"*
> *"Yes. ... No matter who they are we must respect all teachers."*[1]

No teacher should enter the profession and remain in it without hearing these words. It will inspire them to live up to their high calling. No student, school administrator, or public supporter should not recognize the truth of these words. No governing power should restrict the activities and resources they make available to the school as it seeks to fulfill its purpose. In a real sense, everyone in the community should live out this sentiment in word and deed for there is a sacred dimension to schooling that demands that all of us live up to what these words imply.

As we listen to this dialogue between teacher and villager, we are taken aback by the all too frequent sentiment spoken next by the teacher. Surprised, he exclaims:

> *"No-one ever told me that, not even in my training days!"*

It is in the face of such chilling silence about what school really means that this book attempts to raise its voice and proclaim the school a place for respect, protection, caretaking, and reverence. In other words, school is sacred.

Schools are so much with us that we scarcely notice them anymore. But they are very much a part of our lives, whether we are a parent, teacher, learner, or waiting in line behind a school bus with its flashing lights. And the variety of schools—state-supported, charter, parochial, home, Pre-K, elementary, junior high, secondary, technical, special schools for exceptional and challenged students, and online schools, along with academies, community colleges, universities, continuing education institutes, and so on, is ever present. All, or at least most of us, have spent many years of our lives in one kind of school or another.

A danger lurks, however, within this familiarity: we can turn our attention away from the schools and take them for granted. And when we do that, we expose them to dangers from multiple fronts. Today, schools are under duress because society itself is under duress. The cultural, political, religious, and socioeconomic mix that makes up our communities brings stresses and strains to providing an effective education for all because each of these lines of difference, individually and systemically interconnected, make demands and assert priorities that are not commensurable. Equally distressing, in the Western world at large and the United States in particular, ideological divisions can give rise to a spectrum of offensive or even violent actions and reactions to what the school might be doing. Changes promoted by some are loudly resisted by others. Although schools are a part of virtually everyone's experience, we lack a common ground, a body of shared fundamentals for collective planning for education.

But when we think about it, schools in all their forms and sizes have done more to shape our society than most other institutions in the land. The overall population can read, write, and compute because of the schools. The youngest among us have learned their numbers, letters, and colors. While generations of learners have discovered the world and much about themselves, still others have earned their credentials for the workplace, and many have preserved and then pushed out the boundaries of present knowledge in the arts, humanities, and sciences as scholars and researchers. No school has fulfilled its role perfectly because all schools are managed by fallible human beings under imperfect conditions with incomplete and flawed curricula for learners in-process. There are many examples of miseducation where teaching, learning, and what is learned have been all wrong. Yet, most individuals have gained the skills, knowledge, and values needed to function in life as productive and informed citizens. So, while there is always plenty to fault the schools on, and an abundance of reforms we would like to make, there is much more to celebrate about schools than condemn.

These troubled times should provoke us to go back to basics. Tinkering with reforms and making minor adjustments here and there to cope with whatever current issue has to be addressed, or pressing for minor, partial, or partisan victories along the way, will not necessarily bring about long-term solutions. A refreshed philosophy of education, however, can provide grounding for decision-making and action in these times.

Philosophy of Education

Philosophy is not ideology because it is open-minded and self-critical, able to consider alternate viewpoints, and make adjustments as called for. It tends to be iterative in the sense that ideas from past thinkers remain alive in current philosophizing either informing or providing a counterbalance; Plato and Aristotle still enlighten current philosophies in the West, as Confucius does in Chinese thinking, and the seers who composed the *Upanishads* do in Indian philosophy. But it is more than conservative. Past constructions can be thoughtfully dismissed or resurrected and reframed to suit current contexts or woven together in novel ways to provide new insights. Thinking from the last century or beyond is considered in this account because it is foundational and because it can also provide a point of departure. Educational philosophy sits at the cutting edge of imagining what the school can be and do going forward.

An advantage of a philosophical approach to the challenges schools face at this time is that it takes a step back from the messiness of immediate realities to take in a wider view. Such a meta-analysis can wrestle with the central concepts of education regardless of level of schooling or the content of the curriculum or the particular context in which it is being conducted. It interrogates the aims and purposes of schooling, encompassing issues around who should be taught, how the teaching should be undertaken, and why teach at all. This wide scope can focus attention on the fundamentals that undergird the work of the schools across age groupings and subject matter.

Another advantage of a philosophical approach is that it also provides depth as well as breadth in its critical analyses. It digs deeply into basic concepts, unpacking their meaning and examining the glosses and images that color their interpretation. It goes beyond common usage to reveal the fuller meaning embedded in concepts that we might use casually or from habit or even misuse in our conversations. It is a tool for probing the intent and value of whatever is the current fad in schooling. In its role, philosophy clarifies central terms used in education and sharpens interpretations when they are murky.

Philosophy of education, however, is also an applied philosophy. While it does not work with the raw data that might be collected by observation and empirical research in actual classrooms, its analyses and interpretations of key ideas and concepts take into account what teachers and learners are experiencing. Furthermore, while an applied philosophy does not offer precise instructions about how education should be conducted, it does offer practical guidelines that schools can adapt and apply within their particular settings.

Given that a philosophy of education relates closely to the classroom, what we have seen and experienced as an educator influence and inform what we propose as a philosophy. Throughout this account, I have called on actual events and observations from my years as a learner, a teacher, and an administrator in elementary school, high school, college, and university in multiple settings and different countries. I would urge my colleagues in whatever educational setting they might find themselves to do the same and develop a philosophy of their own that is true to what they know and feel in the profession. As Socrates proclaimed at his trial for impiety and corrupting the young, "the unexamined life is not worth living."[2]

Right now, analyzing the concept of the sacred in the context of the school is both timely and fruitful. "The hallowed halls of learning" is as old trope of uncertain provenance. It denotes a place of learning that is respected and revered, maintaining a reputation as a place of knowledge and academic rigor. Unfortunately, it has also come to connote a reverence for schools of high culture, projecting an elitism and privilege for the fortunate few where studies are of the esoteric and intellectual kind. Revisiting the sense of the hallowed, however, can uncover, or better recover, a wholesome appreciation of the sacred nature of school that is free of narrow constructions of worthy students and favored fields of study. Such an approach can open up a possible foundation for understanding and working within education in these troubled times.

In sum, viewing the school as sacred and all that this implies can provide guidance for those engaged in the education enterprise. It can lead to answers about where, when, how, for whom, and why education can and should proceed. It is a foundation of beliefs, a backdrop to planning and action that can inspire and promote our best efforts in teaching and learning.

A Sacred Lens

In exploring the relationship between education and the sacred, one would naturally expect considerable attention to be paid to the teaching of sacred themes in the curriculum, particularly in cross-cultural and anthropological studies, religious studies, and education in literature, music, and other arts. Such themes are usually represented in disciplines that draw heavily on the imaginative and speculative bases of knowledge where myth is implicated as a source of metaphor and ultimately meaning-making or, as Nelson Goodman would say, "world-making."[3]

While I believe this to be true and thoroughly support an education in the arts and humanities (and the artistic and humanistic qualities of the sciences, technology, and mathematics), in this project, I explore the relationship between education and the sacred from a different perspective. I ask what it might signify if the school itself and what happens within it were to be constructed in our collective imagination in sacred terms. And how might we maximize and operationalize this potentiality for the school and the teachers and students who occupy it? In other words, I look at the question not of how or why the school teaches about the sacred, but at how the school itself can be appreciated as sacred. In the end, however, the two questions are not in opposition but may actually be complementary and interdependent.

School is a building, a thing, an object in physical space, but when we consider the *meaning* of school, we resort to using an interpretative lens (or metaphor) or many lenses because this kind of meaning is difficult to express in literal language. Depending on the kind of meanings we pursue in a particular context, we depend on our imagination and pursue possibilities for what a particular image of the school might reveal.[4]

An early lens was offered in the sixteenth century by John Amos Comenius who laid out an explication of what it means when education is seen through the lens of "light," thus reflecting his era, the "age of en-*light*enment." He saw learning driving out the darkness of ignorance at a time when the world of knowledge on all fronts was expanding. With calls to schools and universities to "impart information to all the students on any subject," while those with most potential achieving "encyclopoedic" knowledge,[5] his focus was preeminently on *what* should be taught and that took in the whole world of new information in this age of discovery.

The light lens respects knowledge, knowledge in all the disciplines, but it tends to promote advanced education for an elite few, and overall may be too academic, too removed from preparing learners for daily life when we consider the school today. While we need well-informed graduates with more than a passing acquaintance with the wealth of knowledge that has been generated over the centuries, we also need something that is also relevant to meeting the needs of a multi-layered and more complex world where more than information is required to function well. We also need practical skills, values, attitudes, and the tools for discovering new knowledge.

Despite Comenius's view of "universal knowledge," he did not reckon with the traditions that are non-Western but which are also represented in school populations today and while he lived in an age of rapidly expanding knowledge, his view of what the world knew was largely limited and static by today's standards; he could not foresee the exponential growth in all discipline areas and the new disciplines that are continuing to emerge. This raises the question of whether the "light" metaphor can be stretched sufficiently to meet these current realities.

Sometime later, the Progressive movement, building on Comenius's reforms and initiated by Jean-Jacques Rousseau, recaptured by Friedrich Froebel and Maria Montessori and later by John Dewey and Jerome Bruner, among a host of others, thought of the school through the "garden" lens. The learner is seen as the growing plant, and the instructor the gardener, cultivating, weeding, watering, feeding the plant. It invites us to see the growing child and the older learner in terms of their developmental stage. Teachers expose learners to what they need to flourish: age-appropriate experiences and resources to enable natural growth, captured in the phrases, "learning-by-doing," "discovery learning," or "experiential learning." As the saying goes, the instructor is "not so much the sage on the stage, but the guide by the side." The primary focus of this movement has been on *how* learning happens: naturally, driven by students' curiosity and their present need, and supported by teachers who provide opportunities and resources for discovery.

The garden lens is focused on individual learners, their needs and personal growth; it is democratic and humane, but when learning is largely self-determined, it rests on rhapsodic learning experiences and free choice that might not accomplish all that society requires of its schools. Again, there is a need for something more, something that guarantees a fund of shared knowledge and understanding for the common good.

Imagining the school in terms of a "factory" also has something to offer. It emphasizes the needs of society and its economic stability. It is looking for learners to emerge from their studies able to take their place in the economy as contributing members. Schools are held accountable for the achievement of their students, especially in subject areas where expertise is needed, often referred to as the STEM subjects: science, technology, engineering, and mathematics, and the students' employability. Its central focus, then, is on *what* should be taught with a view to *why* we have schools—to impart the skills and knowledge required for marketplace competence and economic competitiveness.

The factory lens underscores the advantages of seeing the school as a significant contributor to economic stability and growth by training students in professional and practical areas. Unfortunately, the arts—literature, languages, music, aesthetic studies, cultural studies, philosophy, and history, for instance—are often limited or even removed from the curriculum altogether, dismissed because they are seen to have no immediate useful or practical purpose. There is also concern that when there is a job training focus, there is the possibility of encouraging passivity, docility, and uncritical thinking for those destined to be mere workers, along with the objectifying and dehumanizing of the learner it can engender. Again, this metaphor, like the others, has much to offer but in the end is also insufficient because it can neglect the possibility of the non-conformist potential in learners and aspects of meaning-making that are not measurable at a time when accountability is a powerful determinant for what schools should accomplish.

Many metaphors that have shaped our conception of school reflect the mood of society in their day, but they have lingered in our thinking. We can still see some value in seeing the role of the school as enlightening student minds, providing for natural and personal development, or preparing learners for the economic world that awaits them. We can also see that one lens alone is seldom sufficient to capture the whole purpose and role of the school. Each one acts as a corrective to the others while being limited in itself.

The present mood challenges us to bring our imagination to again bear on what image might best meet our times. It will need to reflect our current understanding of the learner, what learning encompasses, how learning happens, and what the schools have to offer the learner and the community at large. It will need to inspire and bring together people across partisan divides by addressing something more than immediate, pragmatic considerations. To do all this, it must capture a vision of the school and the learner in their fullness as we understand them today.

The lens of sacrality, with its variety of features and glosses, takes a very wide perspective. It is inclusive of all levels of education, all subject matter, all learners. It provides guidance for the *what, how,* and *why* of schools as well as the *where* and *when*. Its implications are abundant, as we shall see. It can be, in essence, a grounding metaphor for other metaphors.

My purpose, then, is to explore the deep meaning of the sacred in broad, non-religious terms and what it can offer education in our public imagination. Incorporating but going beyond dictionary definitions, we will examine some foundational thinking about what the sacred is and how it is manifested and nurtured. In drilling down into the sacred constructions of education, it is soon apparent that one enters a vast and multi-dimensional domain encompassing mind, body, and soul. It invites us to examine, for instance, how the curriculum is taught, the design of the school with its entrances, specialized rooms, and their uses; the shaping of schooling within sacred time, its history and traditions, the way it is organized and paced by rituals, and how it serves as a repository of sacred objects and secrets.

Approaching the Subject

To explore the theme of the sacred nature of schooling, I will call on the thinking of educators, historians, anthropologists, and, yes, religious scholars, as well as my own experience. Religious thinkers can contribute to our understanding because they have diligently studied the sacred through centuries of scholarship and practice, and although we may learn from them, we are not compelled to come to traditional religiously constructed conclusions. One of the scholars frequently referenced in what follows is Mircea Eliade (1907–1986), an historian of religions and philosopher. As a founding thought leader in the field of comparative religion, his work is helpful because he attempts to locate and explicate some of the commonalities of the sacred across faith and ethnic traditions, times and places. He provides the discipline with a common language and some fundamental shared notions about the sacred that will be useful for our present purposes.

One of the strengths of Eliade's work is that he examined the wide range of anthropological phenomena available to him through the research of others and his own fieldwork and observations and allowed these phenomena to speak for themselves without trying to explain them in terms of sociology, linguistics, economics, and so on. Eliade interpreted the sacred places, times, and rituals of original peoples as re-creations or models of what they believed were cosmic events involving the gods. While engaging with these symbols of the sacred, these people believed they would participate in the power of what they represented. Only what might be called "remnants," "survivals," or "camouflages" (Eliade's words[6]) of these beliefs remain today, but the symbols are still inherently emblematic. What was once construed more literally as *representations* of the sacred are now likely to be considered more metaphorically as *expressions* of the sacred. That is, for the ancients, the symbols of the sacred pointed to what were believed to be the actual behaviors and intentions of the gods; by participating in them, something of the power of the gods could be absorbed. For us, these symbols are figurative and suggest the meanings and emotions and actions around what is ultimate and most life-affirming. By recognizing them, we can create an understanding of ourselves, the world, and what might lie beyond what is immediately apprehended.

Eliade's critics claim that he was indiscriminately eclectic in his choice of sources, that his interpretations of sacred times, places, and rituals may have been overdrawn and essentialist, even too Euro-centric, and too conservative politically with a nostalgia for a primitive past. His work remains informative, however, because he differentiated clearly between the sacred and the profane, the cosmologically significant and the immediately secular, the existential and the incidental. His writings are voluminous, spanning cultures and times, yet consistent in his elaboration of the meaning of the sacred and its place in human thought. From his oeuvre, we can extract principles and qualities that remain foundational to thinking about the sacred; that is, the sheer scope of his examination of the sacred across times and cultures and the characterizations he developed remain useful tools for analysis.

Incidentally, Eliade's analysis that regards the sacred *sui generis* also permits us to propose that, while the sacred has shaped religious thought and practice, religion does not have exclusive rights to the spiritual nor does a religion guarantee spirituality. In fact, even though many educational institutions sponsored by traditional faiths to serve the particularly religious purpose of grounding their students in a specific tradition, they may not fulfill their potential for sacredness for the sacred transcends the practical realities of schooling and engages the world of meaning and understanding beyond the immediate. The sacred needs to be recognized and nurtured even in religious education settings.

Furthermore, Eliade prompts us to recognize that ordinary usage is not ultimately satisfying as a definition of the sacred. It raises questions about exceptions and omissions that expose the ambiguity and complexity that surround the concept.

The Importance of the Sacred

Alfred North Whitehead concluded his first essay in *The Aims of Education and Other Essays* with a startling statement that has provoked discussion and analysis for a century. He proclaimed that "the essence of education is that it be religious."[7] This claim comes at the end of a serious critique of the curriculum of his day. What students were learning was, he maintained, filling their minds with "inert ideas" that were not only "use less" but "harmful." This "dry rot of the mind" came about, he argued, because knowledge was not being utilized, tested, or combined in new ways but was simply being learned to pass examinations. There was no sense that there was any joy of discovery or a growing understanding "of the stream of events which pours through [the learner's] life, which is his life."[8] He saw a ruinous disconnect between how the subject matter was being studied and "Life, in all its manifestations."[9] He urged schools to "impart an intimate sense for the power of ideas" which has peculiar reference to the life of the being possessing it."[10] What Whitehead termed "religious," in his project, I am naming the "sacred" in this study. In what follows, we will visit the various means of eliciting a sense of the sacred in school but fundamentally they elaborate on Whitehead's idea of connecting learning with self-understanding, meaning, and wisdom, that is, with life itself.

Regarding the school as a sacred space, the years spent there by students as sacred time, and the learning undertaken as a sacred trust will not solve every problem the kindergartens, schools, colleges, and universities face today. It will not prevent every incursion into its unassailable and inviolable space. We should have no illusions that recapturing in our collective imagination the sacred nature of schooling will solve all the problems and challenges of schools today and there will be no more violence in the school, no indifferent learners, no unsupportive community members, no lack-luster teaching, no political ideologues, no angry parents.

On the other hand, these challenges will not be addressed successfully with piecemeal fixes. It requires a foundation of beliefs and imaginings upon which to build solutions, a north star to give direction, a fundamental attitude to guide our decision-making and responses, a deep appreciation of the nature of schooling—and maybe that lies in imagining the school as sacred.

* * *

Thinking of school as sacred gives us as a community the grounds for how we might regard the school. It can be a source of values and a guide for our priorities. It can inspire and help direct our efforts. It can motivate us to do our best for these institutions when so many other needy causes clamor for attention. It is a call to protect, nurture, and promote the schools, the learners within them, and the teachers who lead them toward knowledge and understanding. It demands that teachers and students, their administrators, policymakers, and supporting communities take seriously the sacred responsibility that has been placed upon them.

CHAPTER 2

Exposing the Dark

This may seem like a strange place to begin an account of schooling that aims to be inspiring and positive, whose purpose is to uplift the kindergartens, homeschools, elementary schools, high schools, technical schools, colleges, and universities in our hearts and imaginations. However, we begin here because we see all about us at this present moment in history a darkness that would engulf or at least inhibit all that the schools could offer. Trends toward authoritarianism and anti-intellectualism and inhumanity in society today expose the need for a renewed vision of and commitment to the more optimistic truer potential of education. Proposing such vision is the purpose of this book. The dark and gloomy picture throws into stark relief the possibilities of the contrary. In the ugliness and darkness of sacrilege we may be encouraged to look for its opposite, the sacred with its beauty and light. Here, on the dark side, we may find the impetus to seek out answers and responses to the threats and challenges to what education can really be: celebratory, joyous, and life-affirming. The stresses and strains in society at large are mirrored in the schools, as the schools themselves become staging grounds, even battle grounds, for playing out the tensions in society at large. An account for our time must acknowledge what is troubling education (and by implication the wider community). Once these influences are honestly laid out for review, a renewed vision can emerge to reclaim the standing and promise of education today.

Forces of Desecration

On December 6, 1989, during 20 minutes of terror, a gunman opened the present era of school shootings when he entered the engineering school at École Polytechnique in Montreal, Canada, moved through the corridors, cafeteria, and classrooms, killing 14 women altogether and wounding another 14 before killing himself. On March 13, 1996, a gunman in Dunblane, Scotland carried four handguns and 743 rounds of ammunition into the primary school, shooting randomly into the gym where the kindergartners were taking physical education, then the library, and back to the gym where he took his own life. He left 16 children and their teacher dead and many others wounded, both physically and emotionally.[11] In September, 2004, Chechnyan militants stormed into a school in Beslan, Russia killing 330, most of them children whom they apparently deliberately targeted.[12] At the Child Development Center in Uthaisawan in rural Thailand, an angry former policeman armed with a gun and a knife killed 36 people including 22 children in 2022.[13] In the quiet rural town of Newport, Connecticut, on December 14, 2012, a young man with an assault weapon and a grudge shot his mother at home and then burst into the Sandy Hook Elementary School, where he shot to death 20 five- to ten-year-olds and six school administrators.

Since then, we have seen multiple massacres and no doubt others after these words are published. The record of school shootings in the United States especially has been horrific since the shooting at Columbine High School, Colorado in 1999 and this kind of deranged attack has continued unabated. These horrors have seared in our minds images of children running for their lives with hands held above their heads. To date, the media have not shown us the mangled and shredded bodies of those slain by assault rifles—it might be more than we could bear to see.

We are dismayed that children at school have to practice "shelter in place" drills in case the unthinkable occurs. We have seen these things so many times in the media it has become almost a commonplace.[14] Wherever and whenever children and young people are killed or maimed, we are deeply disturbed and dismayed because we sense on some level that we are inherently entrusted to protect and nurture our young but have failed them. When we gather them into schools and carnage happens, we are even more appalled and aghast, if that were possible. Our horror is even further exacerbated when we learn that in some instances the protections that should be in place have collapsed and children are left to the mercy of a crazed killer.[15]

In these accounts of school shootings, we sense that the school, a place inviolable, invulnerable, inalienable, revered, consecrated, and protected, a place that has been put in our hands as a sacred trust, has been breached. Where has the notion of the "hallowed halls of learning" gone? In essence, school shootings are the antithesis of the sacred; they are abjectly profane. They are, however, just a stark symbol of other potent and more widespread desecrating influences affecting schools today for there are many other instances of the profane escalating in schools.

We have seen faces contorted with anger at school board meetings or at the school gates over health and safety protocols or specific literature, art works, and topics in the school curriculum. Often these outbursts are nothing more than reactions to ideological half-truths and political bias or individual and personal religious belief argued as though their tenets were applicable to all. The disruption and verbal fighting were so bad in some school districts over COVID-19 restrictions and the teaching of race history in the US, for instance, that local school boards had to put in place a list of rules to govern the public's behavior at open meetings to make room for reasoned discussion.[16]

Ideologies from the left or right can stretch behaviors and attitudes to extremes. Enthusiasm for issues around social justice can skew or crowd other subject matter out of the curriculum and omit different yet significant perspectives. A particular theoretical stance, be it postmodernism, critical theory, intersectionality, or post-humanism, can become so dominant that it places itself beyond criticism and develops a blind eye to alternative viewpoints and those who hold them. Language is policed for political correctness and keeping up with "correct" labels and expressions is unremitting. Learners with conservative or religious backgrounds, which are quite legitimate and add to the rich diversity of our communities, can feel uncomfortable when their positions are ridiculed or unwelcome in liberally biased classrooms.

On the other hand, intrusions from the opposite side of the ideological spectrum by the state or local governing boards into what can be in the school library or what topics can be studied, or who will be appointed to boards of overseers and administrations are attacks on some of the fundamental principles of education. The traditional values of academic freedom, freedom of speech, and faculty governance have been essential bulwarks against political and economic intrusions that would breach the sanctity of the institution, but these are now being eroded by some who believe their personal ideology must prevail universally. Questions about curriculum content and faculty rights are fraught with extremist stresses from the right and left of the partisan divide when they should be resolved in favor of providing the best education for all students.[17]

Academic freedom is one of the most significant safeguards of the sanctity of schools. In Europe, the USA, Canada, UK, Australia, South America, and many other countries across the globe, statutes and policies to guarantee this freedom are in place.[18] The American Association of University Professors outlines the primary facets of academic freedom that have been generally accepted as fundamental: teachers are free to research and publish the results of their research; teachers are free to teach and discuss issues in their area of expertise; teachers are free to speak on public matters as citizens and professionals.;[19] and teachers have the right to participate in shared governance.[20] In essence, academic freedom is both a freedom *from* and a freedom *for*. Its intent is to liberate teachers and researchers from government and commercial pressures that would limit or direct what is to be studied or examined as it also permits the educational program to be free to pursue knowledge unhampered by political considerations, opening topics for research or that are related to the content of a course for discussion and critical analysis, and sharing findings without fear of retribution.

Academic freedom has implications across the educational sphere. It grants educators the right to free speech, to share in governance, to develop curricula and how they will teach, and to influence the conditions of their employment. These are the kinds of freedoms and responsibilities that mark education as a profession. Yet, in many schools today, each of these principles is under attack.

The aggression in the Middle East and Eastern Europe brought the issue of free speech on campus into the spotlight.[21] The question about what is acceptable and unacceptable in student protests and faculty members' stances has not always been clear and university leaders and boards of trustees have overridden faculty in introducing restrictions that do not always align with previous, more open policies,[22] sometimes under pressure from government bodies. These actions will long linger in debate on university campuses.

State and local legislatures are removing subject areas and topics from the curriculum, especially in sex education, race history, ethnic studies, and DEI (Diversity, Equity, and Inclusion) and the teachers and administrators who have supported these fields and are replacing them with other faculties. Books have been banned from school and even public libraries along with significant artworks and literatures. Teachers also report that they are assigning fewer books because the world of work opportunities up to and including the "ultimate lifestyle job of being an influencer" does not demand the "intellectual rigor" of reading a whole book and many students have not developed the skill or perseverance to do so.[23] Meanwhile, attempts are made in some regions to mandate that the Ten Commandments be clearly displayed in classrooms and the Bible be included for study not as literature but as faith.

Shared governance by faculty has been subverted in many places, and the appointment of some trustees to governing boards has overridden faculty decisions and traditions. Tenure, underwritten by the principles of academic freedom, although unfortunately sometimes abused, is under threat and in some cases has been removed altogether and some teachers have been dismissed, even "without cause," because supervisors have not agreed with the positions they have taken or the subject matter they teach.[24]

This increasing disempowerment of teachers over the choice of subject matter and the conditions of their employment comes from multiple sources. In the larger picture, the world is experiencing a rise in autocracy and authoritarianism. The pendulum is moving from democratic approaches to governing and problem-solving in a multivocal world to univocal decision-making by dictatorial figures and their supporters. The freedom divide between societies based on democratic principles and those based on autocratic principles widened during the COVID-19 pandemic and was reflected in the different ways governments responded to the crisis with both short-term and long-term results often reflected in more dictatorial and less information-based approaches to problem-solving.[25] The power is moving away from the people to the rulers in a wave of anti-intuitive irony called "populism;" that is, the growing discontent on the part of the many against elitist powers who have ignored their needs, can result, however, in a loss of personal freedom. These trends are reflected at times on the smaller stage of the school.[26]

With all freedoms come responsibilities, which constrain or limit that freedom. A teacher with academic freedom is not free to simply indoctrinate or belittle a learner on the grounds of free speech. A teacher who acts professionally in the school setting is not free to act unprofessionally outside of school.[27] Controversial material should not be introduced into a course if it is not related to the content of the course. Teachers appointed to religious schools or schools with a stated mission may engage their students in critical analysis but are not free to undermine the commitments of the school.[28] While teachers may enjoy the benefits of academic freedom, their students also have this freedom and its accompanying responsibilities. Their viewpoint, if it happens to differ from that of the teacher, should not be dismissed or ridiculed, as many conservative students have reported, but neither does academic freedom for students or faculty permit free speech which supports hate or disrupts the rights of others to attend class or endangers their safety.[29] Ignoring these considerations can also mar the sacredness inherent in education.

Another source that threatens to weaken academic freedom emerges from the implementation of business models of management into the school. Efficiency, productivity, and accountability, all measurable phenomena, become hallmarks of success in corporate thinking. The emphasis is put on measurement, data collection, and evidence-based decision-making, forces that distract from or discourage an endeavor to regard the school in any terms other than objective and pragmatic. While the quantifiable, non-subjective, verifiable, and certain grounds for something conceived of as truth are significant bases for learning, they do not encompass all understanding and awareness.

Utilitarian conceptions of schooling become apparent in some aspects of the present standards movement and the emphasis on useful content. High stakes testing to measure the amount of student learning and focusing on so-called "useful" knowledge can fail the larger mission of education in a number of significant ways. A significant failure is that they do not deal very effectively with the imaginative, intuitive, meaning-making, and other non-measurable aspects of learning. We can establish to what extent students have learned and demonstrated their learning of the body of information assigned and the set of skills to be mastered. This is a necessary but not sufficient criterion for determining the success of the learning program.

Under the domination of the standards movement, the students have no soul, and neither does the school. By that I do not mean that religious commitment is given short shrift, although there are times when it is, but that, in the bigger picture, the values and meanings, hopes and desires, wonder, awe, and amazement, dreams and hopes and fears that learning engenders are too easily ignored. And yet in many ways, these are at the very heart of understanding and wisdom. In the end, business models do not provide well for learning that is not measurable: the growth in wisdom as well as knowledge, development of a wider perspective of who we are and our purpose in life, addressing individual dreams and hopes and fears. All learning can be evocative, but it is often in the interstices of learning facts and theories that the sacred can be encountered and nurtured by judicious teachers.

In the name of efficiency and productivity, corporate management of the curriculum can override professional decision-making by teachers. Prepackaged courses, often online, well-resourced at the development stage and created by course design professionals, are very efficient: once developed they can be reproduced an infinite number of times at little additional cost or effort. Furthermore, they are more likely to bring a measure of quality control from class to class, take advantage of technological and methodological advances that may be beyond an individual class teacher's expertise, and guarantee that the learning meets its stated objectives. Meanwhile, however, the teacher's role is removed from designing learning and meeting individual needs in specific contexts and is largely reduced to monitoring student progress and assessing student work. As artificial intelligence (AI) continues to be introduced into schooling, even those roles may disappear. The temptation for students to simply fulfill the checklist of stated performance objectives increases while the human interaction that can recognize and pursue with learners the moments of serendipitous insight and the opportunity to reflect meaningfully diminishes. Also, in the name of efficiency, more highly paid, experienced teachers can be replaced with non-tenure track and adjunct faculty as a cost-cutting measure, fostering further concern that the quality of learning is affected and deep learning opportunities are lost.

Another trend that grows out of a business model approach to education is that management tends to be top-down. Corporations are generally hierarchical; academic freedom underscores the value of faculty governance. In the business world, employees are expected to conform and cooperate; in schools, freedom of speech and the right to critique and differ from management are protected. Customer satisfaction is actively sought and maintained by business; education's role is not to keep students happy but to promote their growth in understanding and this involves the difficult tasks of evaluating their learning achievements and serving as gatekeepers to entry to the next level of schooling or a profession—with many potentially upsetting effects. More than that, education can be unsettling and disrupt a student's comfort level by challenging old ideas and opening new ways of thinking and being.[30] In a related way, businesses are focused on what sells in preparing learners for the marketplace; in academe, the emphasis is also on the development of life skills, which can be challenging. Under corporate considerations, business managers may choose to reduce the number of courses that probe life issues (history, literature, music and the arts, philosophy) and expand professional studies and science, technology, engineering, mathematics (STEM) studies because they attract "customers." This is evident even in the professional training of future educators. There the focus is often on practical knowledge and skills while the philosophical, historical, and sociological foundations of education, that can orient a learner in the context and meaning of education, its value and role, scarcely appear in course catalogs. For the business world, education is a product that can be manufactured, packaged, sold in pieces, quantifiable, and composed of a series of lock-step actions on the part of the learner; in the academy, education is more likely seen as a process that is organic, developmental, sufficiently flexible to adapt to individual learners and contexts, and often unpredictable as new lines of discovery open serendipitously. The business model and the traditional model in academe are legitimately different since they function in different ways to serve different purposes. The problem, however, is finding ways for both to prevail in an educational setting where fiscal pressures have made it necessary for schools, on the one hand, to manage their resources more efficiently and, on the other hand, to maintain the principles that undergird a good education. Genuine collaboration needs to be pursued so that both the business leaders and the academics respect and allow the role of the other in genuine partnership.[31]

The question that looms large in this study from these developments is to what extent they can be a desecrating influence in the school. One obvious answer is that mandated changes to curricula previously approved and taught by teachers and faculty members can remove courses with the potential to transform learners' sense of self and their appreciation of context and history. These courses can be provocative and disturbing, revelatory, destabilizing, and explosive, but life-changing. And that is where the sacred is located. To take a censor's pen to a Shakespearean play so that students are exposed to bare snippets of the work, or to remove a study of Michelangelo's *David* from the syllabus because it might expose students to what some would presume to be unseemly or unacceptable, or to condemn a book like *Call Me by Your Name* by André Acimanis, the love story between two men, is to rob learners of the transcendent meaning of great art and its power to shape a life, replacing it with a bland and uninspiring predictability.

As a result, teachers can be hemmed about by packaged courses and rules about what they may expose learners to. They know that if they include some expressions in an open class discussion on a controversial matter or some topics in the lesson plan for which they can claim expertise, they can be dismissed. Such constraints may be done in the name of preserving the sacred (that is, what is judged by some to be saving the learner from seeing or hearing something they should presumably not), but in doing so, the teachers can be considered by their learners as inauthentic and even untruthful, and truth itself is shuttered. This is not the school acting in its role as sacred.

While different perceptions about how the schools should conduct their daily work are valued, opinions that are unexamined and uncritically accepted exacerbate conflict and turn the school into a battleground.

The assumption that since everybody has been to school, then everybody knows how schooling should be done ignores the professional development and experience of educators. Overriding expert decisions with state mandates or authoritarian dictates undermines the reverence and reputation the schools may have as sacred places and does little in the long run to resolve differences. Abusive behavior or limitations put on the content of learning by either the right or left in promoting narrow perceptions of the place of education is an act of profanity for it disrespects the sacred ground on which it is enacted, the role of the school as a common good, and all those who occupy this ground as appointed to a high calling.

Another pernicious breach of the sacredness of school can come from a source that has great potential for good: social media and other technological advances. Cyberbullying can penetrate this space that, because it is sacred, is supposed to be inviolate and safe for all. Alarming reports warn us that suicide is the second greatest cause of adolescent deaths in the United States and being bullied or perpetrating bullying has been closely connected to this trend. Almost one in ten 12-year-olds in a U.S. study reported they had experienced or perpetrated cyberbullying. This was defined as "purposefully trying to harm another person or be mean to them online, in texts or group texts, or on social media (like Instagram or Snapchat)."[32] An avatar created by Character.AI has been accused of contributing to the death of a teenager.[33] The impact of cyberbullying can be just as damaging as a madman with a gun in the school. Concerns have also been raised about the connection between social media, attention, and school success.[34]

Schools have yet to explore the range of possibilities and limitations offered by AI. AI holds great promise for good as a tool for developing the knowledge base and applications to problems. It can, however, also threaten what is sacred for the unwary. Noam Chomsky and colleagues raise a warning when they draw attention to the difference between human thinking and AI processes. "The human mind," they explain, "is a surprisingly efficient and even elegant system that operates with small amounts of information; it seeks not to infer brute correlations among data points but to create explanations." These writers cite, for example, the incredible capacity of small children to develop language skills. This entails generating and communicating complex trains of thought from relatively small amounts of data, including grammar and words, instinctively in such a way as to make sense to themselves and others. Their internal "operating system" is simply different from that of the machine and they can do what machines cannot; that is, they can not only describe and predict what is the case, but also say what would not be the case, the ability to distinguish between the possible and impossible, what these writers indicate is the "mark of true intelligence." For scholars, they remind us that AI is a "plagiarizing machine" that "doesn't create anything, but copies existing works, of existing artists, modifying them enough to escape copyright laws." More importantly, they add, AI cannot engage in moral thinking.[35] And we can add that sacred thinking also lies outside the capacity of AI because the pursuit of the sacred goes beyond known facts and data points to what they mean about ourselves, our world, and whatever may lie beyond.

Funding for schools at all levels seems to be a constant challenge for the administration of education. In the US, what were once state-run universities have too often become state-supported institutions facing years of budget cuts from state governments, and administrators spend much of their time and resources away from academic leadership to fund-raising instead. But in seeking alternative sources, institutions may find that churches, foundations, investors, and other sources of financial backing have agendas that can impact the school and its program, putting limits on who can be hired and what can be taught. For-profit schools have brought innovation and efficiency to the conduct of education along the lines of good business practices and can free themselves from dependency on external support, but there are temptations to make a profit over a strict maintenance of academic integrity.[36] We can add that setting tuition costs so high that many potential learners cannot afford college without going into life-long debt, despite what value their education might bring to themselves and their communities, is another threat. Further, citizens who vote against raising school taxes to meet demonstrated need because they have no children of school ages are also damaging. All schools are dependent on financial and other sources outside of the institution and to this extent are vulnerable. Grants for research, funding for special projects, student loans and scholarships, and many other external sources of support are at the whim of political or socioeconomic forces beyond the control of the school. Anything that compromises the greater vision of education for the good of the learner and society at large, however, desecrates the notion of the school.

The list of profanities continues. Schools that fail to enact and enforce policies to protect students against discrimination, sexual abuse, and racial intolerance. Teachers who do not prepare well and offer perfunctory lessons as though they had no calling to be sharers of knowledge and mentors for discovery. Students who fail to exert effort to learn or disparage those who do. In other words, all the members of a community carry a sacred responsibility to nurture the educational purposes of its schools and the needs and aspirations of the learners within them. To do otherwise is to commit sacrilege.

Secularization

Introducing the profane into the school setting is not the only desecrating influence. Secularization also has its impact. In the context of the publicly supported school, it is not the absence of religious instruction that disrupts the sacred. It is rather treating the sacred as though it does not have any power in our lives or any place in our world. It is a way of being in the world where nothing is revered as special and differentiated from the commonplace and banal. In a non-religious sense, this would mean there is nothing that stirs awe and wonder, nothing to be treasured and protected, nothing that inspires nobler living and loftier thoughts, for in its fundamental sense, in these qualities is the essence of the sacred. It is seen in a failure to recognize moments of deep insight and the potential of life-changing possibilities as learners encounter new ideas. It is the absence of time for reflection to explore not only what is becoming known but how the knowing is meaningful on a personal and wider level. So, while profanity is a deliberate destruction of the sacred, secularization is a forgetting or ignoring of the sacred. Both forces make the enterprise of education less appealing, less effective, and less rich and meaningful.

In our present post-Enlightenment, postmodern, and post-human age, many institutions that once shaped life and meaning have become less powerful. Among these, the schools and the whole enterprise of education have largely fallen away from the revered place they once occupied. They bear the impact of pragmatic, economic, and political influences that have secularized them in the public imagination. And yet the old symbols of the sacred and something other than materialistic and utilitarian impulses have not vanished. Can these forces be revived and if so, how could that be done and what would be the end result? In other words, is a resacralizing of education possible and worthwhile?

The Dark Side of the Sacred

While the experience of the sacred can be a communal event, it is at the same time a personal happening, an episode experienced subjectively. What may rise to the level of being sacred to one may not have the same appeal to another. The personal histories of learners will characteristically be made up of pleasant times and happy memories as well as dreads and disappointments. These will play into whether a new experience is received gleefully or fearfully, or as sacred or not. For this reason, an occasion may be received as *mysterium fascinans* for some but for others that same occasion may be primarily *tremendum*. In other words, an encounter that may be repellent or underwhelming for some in the class, can be appealing and even joyously overwhelming (that is, sacred) for others.

Take, for example, the experience of music class for "Philip" and "Lon," respectively. "'Philip,' a bright and energetic eleven-year-old loved music," He had a moment in his clarinet lessons, however, when he could not get more than a squawk out of his instrument. He was sent to a practice room to try alone to get it right but failed. He was offered trumpet lessons instead, but again failed to produce the right sound, and was again sent to the practice room to try alone. His teachers did not know what to do. Unfortunately, he began loitering outside the music studio and leaving his instrument at home.[37] While his classmates may have been breaking through to new joys in music-making and more mature understandings of music, Philip was not. Music lessons were no longer a sacred experience for him.

In contradistinction to this example is that of "Lon." He was a first grader who had already accumulated something of a record at the school: his file, an inch thick, tallied his suspensions, expulsions, and the interventions applied by the school to address his behavioral outbursts. Professor Brenda Brenner, who took her violin students to this school as a service-learning project, described Lon as a "complete hellion." Most of the families represented in this school were transient, poverty-stricken, and many were dysfunctional, and Lon came to school each day carrying this kind of load. The professor took a very different approach to teaching music at this school from what one would expect. These learners were not playing around scratching out pop rhythms anyway they could. They were learning how to stand, how to hold the instrument, how to bow, how to form the notes. They were being taught to regard the instrument and its music as sacred. The simple tunes were drawn from classical literature. When Lon got into the class, he was transformed—he became "a complete angel" and did well in his music class. He rose to the challenge of the discipline and reveled in accomplishing what was set out for him. Unfortunately, in a restructuring of the curriculum when Lon had reached Grade 2, he was reassigned to a beginning music group because of his behavioral record. This did not suit him at all—he wanted to recapture the experience of the more advanced students. He acted out so badly, the security guard had to be called in.[38] Unlike Philip, he knew he found his bliss in his music class. This was his personal sacred space.

In the larger picture, we see that the sacred is a differentiator, separating the hallowed from the profane by drawing a boundary around special moments and places and actions. However, drawing distinctions between different conceptions of what is sacred and what is not should always raise the question: What (or who) is included and what (or who) is left out?[39] Much rests on how this question is answered.

A dark note in considerations of the sacred as a differentiator is the possibility that the perspective taken by a few may set them apart from others and potentially create an elitism that can lead to disparaging others.

In the general public, the labels "liberal" or "conservative" are very effective at doing more than simply dividing people from each other—they can create mutual condemnation or denunciation between partisans, neighbors, and fellow citizens of different persuasions. Closer to the school experience, the football team may be lauded while the nerdy student is ridiculed or vice versa. When this happens, the sacred can become a weapon for sorting who is acceptable from who is unacceptable. Further, a sense of exclusiveness may destroy or dissuade another from embracing a potentially sacred moment because they may start from a position of feeling too alienated to participate.

When learners are taught to discriminate against another or even worse despise another, when they are led to believe from what they have picked up from their schooling that they have rights and prerogatives above their neighbors without corresponding responsibilities or when they fail to learn not only the stories told by winners but also those of the losers, the word sacred can be invoked for the curriculum, but it may connote protectionism.

Equally negative, a particular sense of what is sacred may provide grounds for impelling others to join in even though that experience of the sacred has no attraction to them. A measure of imperialism can be implied or subtly enforced in the name of unity or school spirit. One thinks, for instance, of the Jewish singers in the school choir preparing a Christmas program with carols and hymns. They may even sing with as much gusto as their classmates but unobtrusively choose to mouth the word "Lord" when it comes along rather than give it voice. It is an uncomfortable experience for them especially if no recognition or reason or even allowance is given for what might feel like an imposition. An informed balance in perspectives taught can help alleviate the argument that one set of ideas or one ideology prevails and is imposed on learners during their educational experience. Exposure to multiple perspectives demands respect, coupled with critical thinking, can be a corrective to narrow thinking and promote responsible living together. Even so, given the range of histories and commitments already present in a group of learners, one realizes that an experience of the sacred can be invited, initiated, or nurtured, but should never be forced.

History is replete with times when the sacred has been a cloak not for the transcendent possibilities it can inspire toward the good, but for evil. Laws that allow some to exploit others have been regarded as inviolate. Walls have been built around actions, properties, and people that kept the evil in and unexposed. People cloaked in holy robes, figuratively and literally, have failed to live up to their high calling. Among these possibilities, we might include dearly held hazing and other initiation rites that have been damaging and sometimes fatal. Being declared sacred in itself does not make something good and positive.

One of the darkest sides of the sacred occurs when something that falls short of being worthy or is at worst destructive of worth is regarded as sacred and consecrated. Money, property, or status may be elevated in a materialistic society but since they are transitory and self-indulgent, their veneration does not satisfy in the long run. One's looks, skills, or celebrity may be idolized but these too are eventually found to be hollow. Thoughtful schooling will encourage students to reflect on who are the "heroes" and why, who should be "heroes" and why.

In this same vein and even more pernicious are the ideologies built on narrowly constructed or misinterpreted premises about concepts such as country and patriotism, free speech, religious freedom, one's socioeconomic class, or geography, for instance. Accepting white supremacy as sacrosanct, and further, taking it to be a license to bring violence into the public square against non-white others is an insidious evil despite being revered by its adherents. Taking a stance against a whole ethnic group based on wrongheaded views of genetic inferiority or the evil perpetrated by some in a group divides communities on campus and off. It can be an abrogation of the sacred right to responsible free speech as well as being a threat to the continued presence of different others. A commitment to the idea that we own nature and its resources and can exploit them for our advantage is another malicious elevation of an ideology that is unworthy of nurture and reverence. Such devotions bring harm, destruction, and even death to those who glorify them and sadly also to others. Critical reflection as individuals and societies on what is considered sacred is a vital role for teachers and, by extension, us all.

* * *

In essence, forces have been slowly eroding the sense that schools are hallowed places, set apart and respected, enabled in fulfilling their role for the common good, protected, and nurtured. Assaults have come from multiple directions: external forces that would pierce the sacredness of the school violently, ideologically, technologically, fiscally, and managerially; internal failures that do not grasp the possibilities of teaching for wisdom and meaningfulness as well as knowledge; and the destructive misconstruals and misapplications of the sacred itself. Laying these out for review, and there are others beside, opens the way to imagine how schools can reclaim their sacredness.

What is meant by the sacred has been implied throughout this discussion. Now we can unpack more explicitly what the sacred might be in the context of education.

CHAPTER 3

A Place for Feeling

Many common words defy definition: music, love, hope, meaning, time, feeling, beauty, pornography; even simple words like color. We can talk about these words and insert them into our conversations, and we trust that basically others understand us. But when pressed for their definition, we often resort to saying, I know it when I see, or hear, or feel it.

The "sacred" can be such a word. In the setting of a publicly funded school, however, one must ask more insistently, what does "sacred" mean in this context? This is a particularly fraught question since the most common definitions of the word sacred seem to connect it irretrievably to religion. The *Merriam-Webster Dictionary*, for instance, reflects this common usage by opening its definition with "dedicated or set apart for the service or worship of a deity ..." and continues with "worthy of religious veneration" and "of or relating to religion."[40]

In the US, the "wall of separation between church and state"[41] is a constitutional fundamental, so while teachers in public schools may teach about the religions they are prohibited from teaching religion itself and even then, that may give rise to parental outcries. Suspected incursions into and erosions of this fundamental are hotly contested in public debates and legal battles. Should religious clubs be allowed as extracurricular activities for students in public schools?[42] Should the biblical creation story be added to the science curriculum as a viable alternative to evolutionary theory?[43] Can priests, rabbis, imams, or other religious clerics be permitted to offer religious education instruction in classrooms during the school day or even out of school hours?[44] Can students wear religious clothing to school such as a hijab or even a tee-shirt bearing a religious message or symbol?[45] Can the school music program include religious music for study or performance,[46] or the art class study religious works?

All of these questions are complicated by the fact that in public schools today one finds students of every ethnic and racial group, all of them bringing their own distinctive and incomparable religious perceptions and commitments. Whose religious preferences should be consulted and honored? And what of those young people with no religious affiliation at all? All these questions and the heated sentiments that they stir may tempt one to wonder whether the word "sacred" should be used in the context of publicly funded schooling at all.

However, *Merriam* continues the definition of "sacred" with "unassailable, inviolable" and then "highly valued and important, a sacred responsibility." Another dictionary adds "regarded with reverence," "properly immune from violence, interference," "derived from *sacren* to consecrate."[47] A thesaurus includes in its list of synonyms words such as "inviolable, protected, sacrosanct, secure, hallowed, inalienable, invulnerable, inviolate, unalterable."[48] It is these related but different meanings of "sacred" that prompt us to think of schools as sacred. Recognizing the sacred nature of the schools of the land reminds us that they are a trust given to us to protect and revere for the good of the learners as well as the good of the community. It is this set of meanings that bring the sacred nature of the schools into focus.

It is clear from the concept of sacred that the term sacred used here is not a synonym of the term "religious." While not denying the capacity of religion to open one up to the sacred, to identify and name the sacred, and develop theologies, rituals, and other symbols to explicate the sacred in particular terms, there is also a non-religious experience of the sacred that is relevant to our discussion here. Sam Keen suggests that even though our knowledge may be limited to our experience, our horizons are not. That is to say, a sense of the sacred, as represented by the wider meaning of "sacred," can open up new vistas and levels of meaning for everyone. It is not restricted to the religious life but is a human experience for people of all faiths and non-faith.[49] It is "an unconscious dimension of modernity,"[50] often evoked in our experiences and the way we talk about them.

We all have had memorable instances that were something other than familiar or commonplace, because they provoked us to ponder; they felt sacred to us. When I stepped into the Grand Mosque in Cordova, Spain,

I took in the rows of Moorish arches stretching it seemed into infinity in every direction with occasional rays of light streaming into that semi-dark and silent expanse. I recognized at once that I was in a strange and different place from any I had experienced before. Then a choir at that moment began a Gregorian chant. I was overwhelmed with the sense that I was standing on holy ground. The sights and sounds in that capacious, exotic place were captivating and pregnant with a significance I could feel even if I could not give it words. I had a similar sense of the sacred when I was in Patagonia and looked out from an icy fiord to a mountain range with its hanging valleys and glaciers rarely seen by human eyes all on a scale that was breathtaking. The impenetrable silence and proportion of that magnificent sight were enthralling. For me, this also was a sacred moment.[51]

Not all moments are as stunning or rare as these two examples were for me at that time. Other instances may be as simple as hearing an owl call in the night, or holding a new baby for the first time, or glimpsing a field of wildflowers in bloom, or catching a song on the radio. It makes us stop and wonder. And it need not be a moment of silent awe; it may in fact happen while we stand in a cheering crowd, or hear an orchestra performing music that stirs us, or play in a garage band, or are caught up in the hustle of a classroom of learners actively engaged in creation or experimentation. All these moments may make us catch our breath and take us to a different dimension of awareness. We may not be able to define the sacred, but we know it when we experience it, or better yet, feel it.

Just as defining the word sacred defies literal words, so too it is nearly impossible to describe the feelings in those personal moments when we have a sense of something being sacred. This is due in part to the fact that these experiences are not simply intellectual. In large part, the definitions of the sacred appeal as much or even more to the emotions than they do to thought. Respect, reverence, inviolate, hallowed, sacrosanct, and valued all rest heavily on feeling. Sacred moments, then, are likely to be fraught with feelings as well as with thoughts. In fact, most of our conscious life of thought is powered by our emotions along with bodily sensations and our reconstructions of them. In the realm of the sacred, feeling is more fundamental, so much so that much of what we may say about what the sacred is comes down to talk about what we feel.

Contemporary thought reminds us that mind and body and soul function as one. Unfortunately, the division of human nature into parts has tended to elevate some aspects above others—the mind usually—regarding it as the dominant determinant of what school learning is about. At the same time, the emotional or soulful aspects of human experience have been shrouded in distrust for fear that subjectivity and feeling would distract from the objective pursuit of truth and knowledge. The exploration of emotions in the life of thinking and the impact of socially and physically based emotion dispel those doubts when it is clear that feelings are essentially involved in all meaning-making.

In other words, feelings are inextricably interwoven with living in all its manifestations: the mind, the soul, and the body. That is, they are embedded in the cognitive, affective, and psycho-motor domains, to borrow from Benjamin Bloom's taxonomy.[52] Such a taxonomy exposes the wide range of being human, many elements of which can be overlooked or forgotten altogether: comprehending and evaluating, responding and valuing, and sensing and doing. The original taxonomy itself has undergone some revisions and while the cognitive domain has remained popular, the other two domains are not as central in educational thought. Yet, the broad outline of the taxonomy, with its three domains, provides a useful tool for analysis. In this endeavor, however, we should keep in mind that the taxonomy may tempt us to see life in fragments when in the experience of living, not only do the three domains merge and fuse, but the feelings that accompany them also come together, or as Amanda Williamson expresses it, feelings for the sacred are "body-mind-soul-centric."[53] In what follows, we will explore the cognitive, social, and physical sources of and responses to sacred emotions in the context of education.

Cognitive Feelings

In education, there has always been a focus on the mind alone—what can be learned, stated, comprehended, utilized, enunciated, recalled, expanded, associated, applied, tested. There has been a general wariness of emotions on the assumption that they hamper the pursuit of objective knowledge. Whole learning, however, requires awareness of the feelingful as well as the intellectual.[54] An exclusive focus on the mind overlooks the effect of feeling for the emotions influence our thinking by coloring what we know, what we want to know, what we remember, how we remember it, and what meaning it carries for us.

Not only are emotions present whether we acknowledge them or not, they are indispensable to thinking. They can serve the purposes of education when they are recognized and allowed. Israel Scheffler expanded this line of thought by identifying five emotions, he calls them "cognitive emotions," that accompany and may even empower learning.[55] He exposes the fundamental role of emotion in even the most rational and objective of human pursuits, the sciences, which not only engender feelings but are also thoroughly dependent on them.

First, he reminds us that the scientific enterprise absolutely relies on honesty in collecting data and reporting results. It demands of scientists and other researchers an unshakable love for accuracy in logic and fact. At its best, it also requires respect for different visions because an open, sincere assessment of alternatives can lead to new discoveries. Scheffler calls this collection of cognitive emotions *rational passions* to indicate that rational thought can only be sustained if its participants are passionate about these values.

Another cognitive emotion Scheffler labels *perceptive feelings*. These are emotional responses that guide critical thinking. That is, when someone is involved in a rational endeavor, he not only knows when something is right or wrong, but senses whether it is a good fit or not. This is also where the moral dimension can be invoked. Because a discovery can lead to new applications, the question becomes whether or not it should be pursued.[56] The feeling one has about the direction one should take and about the significance of one's findings are part of the critical assessment of the undertaking.

Scheffler identifies a third cognitive emotion, one that appeals to the more light-hearted yet serious side of scientific work: *theoretical imagination*. This points out the role of playful speculation about the source of new ideas or how they may be applied in problem-solving. It discards strictly formulaic thinking and throws what might seem crazy ideas into the mix in the hopes that they might just create an opening worth pursuing. This is a break from the strictly objective approach to discovery and admits into the process a more subjective, fanciful element.

These three emotional aspects of thinking–rational passions, perceptive feelings, and theoretical imagination–are tools or means to ensure trustworthy knowledge and the production of new lines of investigation and discovery. When recognized for their significance, they can be nurtured both by what we teach and how we teach it.

They also have significant roles to play in the development of the sense of the sacred. We would want claims based on an experience of the sacred to be acceptable to ourselves and others because they are honest, open to correction or modification, appeal to us because they match and may even expand our experience and understanding of the world and our moral values, respectful of alternative claims, and imaginatively and creatively constructed and reconstructed to enhance their meaningfulness as new experiences add further insight.

In considering the realm of the sacred, however, there remains a sense of something more than emotionally governed cognition admits. In this realm, we encounter a different dimension of human knowledge. It does not give rise to facts, theorems, propositions, certainties, or even theories, but it still results in a form of knowing, in this case, an understanding of ourselves, the world we live in, and our place in that world. Parker Palmer speaks of the "eye of the mind" which deals with facts and reason and of the "eye of the heart" that sees other realities. "Either eye alone is not enough. We need 'wholesight.'"[57] This other way of knowing is a source of values and meaning, arenas where rational thinking alone falls short but are of vital significance in living. Where Scheffler's cognitive emotions trace the influence of emotion in directing reason in rational thought, the pathway in this alternative is more likely from feeling to meaning. Understanding in this realm depends on and is centered on emotion.

The concept of "cognitive emotions," then, raises the possibility of a set of corresponding "emotional cognitions" that might be a helpful way to think about the experience of the sacred. It prompts the question of whether there is a form of knowing that arises from the life of feeling, just as there are feelings that arise from and persist in the life of rational thought.[58] Fundamentally, it asks if knowledge can be generated by emotion, what kind of knowledge is it?

The emotional cognition paralleling Scheffler's rational passions might be *expressive information*, that is, insights that arise from experiencing an emotion. Empathy, for instance, allows us to better discern the circumstances of others than the data about them alone might afford; fear may alert us to a real danger; hope may encourage us to look for solutions; experiencing the sacredness of a school may stimulate us to consider our roles in and responses to education in a new way. Recognizing an emotion, reflecting on its possible array of consequences, and sorting priorities to satisfy personal goals are among the important realizations an emotion may produce. Without feelings about something we may not be motivated to think about it at all.

Scheffler's identification of perceptive feelings, that is, emotional responses that can guide reason, may be twinned with what can be called *passional knowledge*, that is knowledge that arises about our emotions. When we think about our inner life of feeling, we come to understand ourselves more fully. The thinking is about the emotion itself. Why am I angry? Should I be pleased about this? Do I have good reason to feel this way? How can I channel this feeling in productive ways? What can I do to stop feeling this way? Why do I have this attachment to my old school? What do I like about history books? When we ask these kinds of questions about our life of feeling we can grow in self-understanding and appreciation for who we are and what direction we want to take in the next steps or life itself. We can come to understand ourselves and others more intimately and authentically.

Critically reflecting on our emotions also opens us to realizing that undisciplined passions can become fanaticism or hardened into a narrow ideology or dogma, excluding alternatives and limiting a fuller awareness of the rich possibilities that might be accessed with more controlled sensations. Blind emotion is rarely healthy or good.

Imaginative reconception can serve in the emotional domain as the counterpart to Scheffler's theoretical imagination in the rational domain. Both employ the imagination, but where the latter pursues new theory through playful speculation about the data, imaginative reconception remakes old understandings about what is felt. This process starts from how something is experienced and builds out understanding from there. Underscoring reconception implies that it may be a matter of seeing the well-known and common in a different way. The familiar assumes a freshness that can have a new depth of meaning. In an important sense, this emotional cognition suggests that the experience of the sacred may arise in the here and now; that is, its origin may lie in the familiar and everyday as well as in the grand and powerful, or what Lynda Sexson has described as the "ordinarily sacred,"[59] yet it may take us to a new realm or level of meaning.

Deeper Connection Between Thought and Feeling

Scheffler goes on to describe two additional emotions that he sees as specifically cognitive. They are cognitive emotions in the fullest sense of the word because they arise from cognitive activity.

The joy of verification, he suggests, comes about when what one predicted, based on previous knowledge and following the cues along the way without presumption, turns out to be actually or sufficiently true.[60] Testing one's hypotheses is one of the most significant tasks in a scientific or rational project. It views an assumption from multiple angles and in different contexts. Until there is sufficient evidence to support a claim, the claim itself is not to be trusted. Even the supporting evidence has to be critically appraised. But when a claim holds up under intense scrutiny, there is a great feeling of satisfaction, even joy.

The counterpoint to joy in Sheffler's analysis is the *surprise* that comes when the effort to verify a finding fails. The finding must be in some way faulty and untrustworthy. While many scientists would justifiably feel despair at this, Scheffler redeems the moment by labeling the feeling more positively as "surprise," because it is evidence of the "rational passion" for honesty, integrity, and open-mindedness. A false finding at the end of a search, even when it is unexpected, is nevertheless a finding: instead of ruling some conclusion in, it rules it out. It can provoke the search for truth in an alternate direction, forcing one to look for an altogether different ending.[61]

In his autobiography, C. S. Lewis recalls a moment in his experience that came as a surprise and a lesson.[62] He had been collected at the train station by his new teacher and on the way to his new school, Lewis casually remarked that the scenery they were passing through was "wilder" than he had imagined. Teacher Kirk, aptly nicknamed the Great Knock, called "Stop! right there." On what basis had such a comment been made? Had the young Lewis seen maps of the area, or photographs, or read any books about the local geography or topology? Of course, he hadn't—he was simply trying to make conversation. "Do you not see," Kirk stated, "you have no right to have any opinion whatever on the subject?" Over time, Lewis did not see his teacher waiver from demanding evidence and ever more reliable evidence for any assertion. Some of the students did not warm to this at all, but for Lewis, that initial shock of discovering the paucity in his thinking was "red beef and strong beer," that is, over repeated teaching moments like this, he came to recognize and welcome the reasonable, evidence-based, and rational, especially when summoned by the shock of discovering that his thinking had been less than absolute about something.

The truly emotional cognitions, the joy of verification and surprise at falling short of a dependable conclusion, are emotions that come as a result of actively engaging in the learning process. They are responses to discovery and serve as a foundation for future learning episodes. They are outcomes and can be acknowledged and celebrated. All five of the cognitive emotions are embedded in the rational enterprise and point toward finding the kind of knowledge that is factually reliable, verifiable, and certain.[63]

There is joy and surprise too in a sacred moment. Where the scientist's emotion comes at the end of a line of inquiry into truth, in a sacred setting they are more likely to come as a surprise at the beginning of an experience in meaning-making. In the sacred realm, the surprise and joy may be dramatic or startling, jolting us into a new world of understanding and meaning, toward a fuller appreciation of what is of value, a better sense of oneself, others, and the world. It is more likely to provoke the sense that one is on the cusp of a new and impelling journey in self-understanding and less like the shock of coming to a dead end. Such an experience at its height is sometimes referred to as a Damascan experience,[64] or an epiphany. A scientist's finding may provide the foundation for another related inquiry, but a sacred insight provoked by surprise or joy itself may mark the start of fresh meaning-making, both pivotal and transformative.

In a sense, the emotions themselves may be both the drivers and the goal in the quest for understanding. This is well represented in a common motif in the Jerusalem faiths: the enclosed or hidden garden, the *hortus conclusus*.[65] It recalls the Garden of Eden, the ultimate paradise, and captures the sense that having once glimpsed it, the pilgrim is always yearning for it, searching for it. Experiencing the sacred is a quest searching to find that place again; "faith seeking understanding."[66] Lewis adopts this figure as an allegory for his own experience. He tells of John, a young man whose imagination had been filled with rules to obey and pits of snakes to avoid, who, out walking one day, happened on a stone wall with a window in it. He could hear a strange sound, like one note of a bell but even further away than a star. He glimpsed through the window and saw a green wood full of primroses. Beyond the wood, through the mists, he saw the sea and an island where nymph-like creatures sat in green chairs. As he reached out toward it, "there came to him from beyond the wood a sweetness and a pang so piercing that instantly he forgot" everything else. He knew that what he had seen was different from anything he had ever seen before and for the rest of his life he wanted to grab it greedily or whatever remained of it once the image faded from his mind.[67] One may have just a peek into something extraordinary that delights and surprises. Even a passing glance into the garden is pure and unexpected enchantment. It can be so inspiring, it spurs one on to further searching and exploration.

Under the tutelage of Kirk, Lewis was also introduced to, or rather immersed in, this other, imaginatively and emotionally created world. With minimal preparation, he sank into the Greek classics so totally he even began to think in Greek.[68] Supplemented with other literature, this was an encounter with the mysterious, awe-inspiring, and transcendent. He recalls his great joy in this fanciful other world. It is similar to how some learners are drawn to music, art, poetry, and literature—through these they may experience both joy and surprise that urges them forward searching new levels of understanding or appreciation. Similarly, it may also explain why some learners pursue sports, science, technical classes, or any of a number of activities or any particular subject in the school curriculum with great devotion, not so much because these amuse or are merely useful for the learner, but because there is delight and meaningfulness in them, a forceful attraction. This is not about happiness in the moment, but about understanding, and a feeling for and wanting something more.

Relational Emotions

Lewis's reminisces about his school and his teacher Kirk also draw attention to the role of the social context in learning. Not all, in fact, very little understanding takes shape within the mind of an individual, figuring things out for herself. The environment in which knowledge grows—other people (family members, friends, teachers, peers, heroes, leaders), the prevailing culture, the traditions of inherited thought, the possibilities the situation presents—play a crucial role in mental development. That is to say that the solo thinker is also a member of a group with common understandings that are fostered and sustained by social interaction. We each bring to a shared culture our own predispositions and potentialities, but by participating with others, we come to absorb and help shape the beliefs as well as the values, attitudes, and commitments of the culture. Together, the group constructs its ideas and meanings about itself, the world at large, and what may or may not lie beyond it, not only from objective inquiry, hypothesis testing, evidence collecting, validating, and proving, but also from learning from each other at particular places and times.

Social constructivism, the theory that captures the role of the social environment on the development of knowledge, expands human learning beyond the rational and scientific.[69] It helps to explain why individuals within ethnic groups, regional communities, generations within a family, political parties, and peer groups think alike—they are constructing their world views and specific understandings together, reinforcing each other. In an educational setting, the teacher's role is both a deliberate instructor and someone who sets the environment for learning which takes into account the part played by the family, community members, and other learners. Explicit teaching may be happening, but a primary vehicle for sharing knowledge is less formal and happens when group members work, play, and socialize together.

When learners move from one environment to another, one mini-culture to another broader one—say, when they move from home to school, or high school to college—they may experience some disorientation until new understandings are absorbed from the larger group and as their own participation begins in turn to contribute to the group's understandings.

The focus of social construction is on the development of cognition, but it is obvious that the processes involved in the social construction of meaning are not only building knowledge alone, but that knowledge is loaded with emotion. In a small way, I saw this happen on the first day of my first teaching appointment in a one-teacher school in a rural and rather remote and isolated community. I was entering the new mini-culture of the school, my new role, and this town and its environs largely unknown to me. In this place on the edge of the Australian Outback, I was soon to learn of the local deep reverence for water and the sanctity of the irrigation schedule, the alert appreciation of the weather reports, the value of mateship and helping one's neighbor in this very ethnically diverse community made up of successive waves of immigrants over the decades, the love of the land, the local football and Dixie band heroes, and the hopes and fears provoked by the weekly market reports.

Closer to my experience of those first moments, I was likely more anxious than I needed to be but determined to make this appointment a success. I was somewhat overwhelmed and unsure as I watched my students line up for class for the first time. But I was not the only one. Jonathan was leaving the K-2 setting and moving into Grade 3 with its different desks and placement in the room, his big brother had just moved onto high school, and now he was confronted with a new teacher. He was feeling very alone. To this day, I remember his words to me as the students came back into class after lunch break: "More of your horrors this afternoon, I suppose!" Our social environment at that moment, where our constructed past did not seem to match our present realities, showed us both that we needed to build anew not only our knowledge base, but our affective responses to this situation and to each other. Fortunately, that came to pass. A few months later, we were working on a cooking project and each of the class members brought the ingredients to school. Jonathan carried in his school bag the makings in separate baggies: the flour, salt, sugar, and so on, all labeled at home, even the wrapped egg. He was so excited by the prospect of trying something new. Together we and the other learners had been constructing a new emotional reality as we interacted. Interestingly, I learned a great deal from the students and their families about living and being a community member in that place, its mores and attitudes and what it valued, and hopefully the pupils learned from the lessons I shared with them. Our experienced emotions contributed to what we knew, and what we were learning together helped to direct and shape our emotional lives.

One element of Lev Vygosky's view of the social construction of knowledge that has been particularly helpful in conceiving the teacher's role in cognitive development is the notion of the "zone of proximal development." In simplest terms, this zone is the distance between what the learner can potentially know and what she currently knows. The teacher and others, including peers, by providing the right kinds of learning situations, can guide the learner in narrowing this gap.[70] While the primary focus here is on developing a learner's cognitive abilities, this is not achieved solely as a scientific course of action, but one that involves language and other forms of communication in social interactions. Furthermore, the experience of reaching toward one's fuller potential is not a solely or even hardly an objective experience, for it is imbued with aspirations, disappointments, joys, doubts, fears, hopes, satisfactions, resentments, attractions, and surprises. As we shall see, the very act of narrowing this gap between potential and reality can be significant not only for cognitive development but also for the affective development of the feelings of the sacred.

The Body and Emotion

The body knows in its own way: there is muscle memory, kinesthetic awareness, and responses to environmental conditions, for instance. The body also provides information to the mind and vice versa so it is nearly impossible to distinguish the specific contributions of mind from body in instances of *knowing how* (that is, practical knowledge or expertise) as distinct from *knowing that* (or descriptive, propositional knowing).[71]

A learner can be highly motivated to perfect a skill: a flawless joint in woodworking shop, a layup in basketball, data collection in the lab, a particular sound from their instrument, a flawless poem, the solution to an algebraic equation. All of these aspirations demand focusing the mind. They draw on anticipated satisfaction and the joy of accomplishment or the disappointment of failure. All are learning moments that bring everything about the actor to bear on the task at hand. A person's physicality can both generate knowledge and feeling and express what is known and felt. In other words, the learner is wholly mind, wholly soul, wholly body.

When Liesl van der Merwe and John Habron studied the phenomenon of spirituality, they analyzed recent writings in music education. They did not interrogate people who have what they consider to be spiritual experiences, but they undertook a document analysis of philosophical and theoretical writings about such experiences.[72] From this analysis, they pose a conceptual model of spiritual experiences. Using Max van Manen's construction of "lifeworld existentials" (corporeality ["lived body"], relationality ["lived human relation"], spatiality ["lived space"], and temporarility ["lived time"]) as the theoretical framework for the study,[73] their analysis reveals that indeed experiences of the sacred include such elements as bodily sensation, social and personal connections, and particular senses of space and time.

As they unpack the notion of "corporeality" in the model, they discover what they consider to be four distinguishable facets. *Embodiment* underscores the phenomenological fact that without a body, there would be no thinking, feeling, or acting; in other words, experience of the sacred, like all experience, is embedded in the body. *Sensory experience* acknowledges that "all sensation comes and is felt and lived" through the body and is a "consequence of what is happening in our bodies and brains." *Creativity*, linked to spiritual "states of ecstasy and transcendence," involves bodily action. Finally, *breath*, which has strong links to Eastern spiritual practices, has also been etymologically related to "spirit" since Roman times. The essence of a living person is "spiritus-breath."[74] While some aspects of these body-spirit facets can appear a little tenuous or vague, the overall effect of the study establishes that something of the human encounter with the sacred is at least a physical phenomenon and that the encounter is not only meaningful but also emotional.

Another view of the embodiment of the sense of the sacred is offered by Deanne Bogdan in her double-sided tool for analyzing feeling in the realm of the sacred: the "shiver-shimmer" factor.[75] This duality is the foundation of her discussion that the emotions making up our response to the sacred are embedded in the body. Where the shiver suggests the impact of incoming emotional stimuli, the shimmer suggests the response to those stimuli, and both are inextricably implicated in the physical.

The "shiver factor," she proposes, is the very physical response of emotion, the "fingers up and down the spine feeling." She draws her analysis from music, but her conclusions are not limited to the aesthetic field. A history student viewing the real Magna Carta, a math student finding the solution to a problem that was so elusive, the new reader who completes his first whole book, or the geography student who sees with new eyes the flood plain and delta near her home can have the same shiver experience as a piano or voice student. These shiver experiences may be as simple or life-shaping as the shock of awareness of something new or a novel perspective on the familiar or the surprise that comes from an encounter with the unexpected. Bogdan reminds us that in the educational context, these kinds of very real bodily reactions should be acknowledged, reflected on, and subject to critical review.

The "shimmer factor" begins as the "instinctual and instantaneous apprehension of" what has brought about the emotion and culminates in an imaginative embodiment of understanding that is deeper than simply intellectual because it ensues in an action response. I see this as a taking into oneself what the emotion implies for both meaning-making and doing. When we enter a sacred place, for instance, and realize where we are, our deportment changes. Depending on the circumstances, we don a scarf or remove a hat, we may kneel or bow or stand to attention. When Moses encountered the burning bush that did not seem to be consumed, he was compelled to remove his shoes for he sensed he was standing on holy ground—an event that has become an icon of feeling and action in the presence of the sacred. The incident marked his acceptance of his calling to lead his people out of slavery.[76] As a young person and a member of my church's youth club, we would recite the pledge at each club meeting. To this day, I remember an item in the pledge: "To walk softly in the sanctuary." So too, our behavior inside the school is different from that in the playground. Teachers often use the expression: "We use our 'inside' voice in here." The bodily experience of feeling may spur us to try harder or reach out with new understanding to another. And undergirding these actions is a deeper understanding of the sacred and our relationship to it.

We should keep in mind, too, that there is often reticence to approach the sacred physically out of respect for it—and that too is a bodily action. High into the facade of the Nidaros Cathedral in Trondheim, Norway is the sculpted figure of a mason holding the last brick for the building in his hand. In front of him in the wall is a brick-shaped space ready to be filled. But the mason hesitates forever before that space. The myth around the figure is that if the last brick is cemented in place, bad things will happen; the fiord will fill, and the town will flood. The image of the uncompleted or imperfect task is echoed around the world. A scholar from Japan explains how a gilded vase must not be perfect but bear some mark of human error,[77] and an Australian friend recounts how her grandmother and great aunts always left a small part of their embroidery unfinished for the same reason. The perfect is inviolate and should not be carelessly and bodily approached although emotionally drawn toward it. The resistance to claiming or appropriating perfection embodies both the shiver of emotion and the shimmer of understanding it and acting accordingly.

* * *

A rounded learning is comprised not only of cognition but also of the emotions and physical actions and social interactions that are necessary guides for it and expressions of it. In the intellectual realm, the honesty, respect, and passion for accuracy, emotional responses that direct critical thinking, the imaginative free play of the mind, the joy of verification when found to be right, and the surprise at being found to be wrong, are all indispensable. It also means acknowledging the role of reason in the emotional life and the reason-filled results of emotional responses to learning–the emotionally embedded insights into self and one's relationship with everything else, rationally disciplined emotions for trustworthy conclusions, imaginative reconstructions of our ideas to plumb for meaningfulness, and practicing a skill to improve it. It means too seeing that some emotions, like joy and surprise, are consequences of learning something new or doing something better than before, and on other occasions the pivotal moment for seeking deeper and more meaningful understanding. And throughout, emotions and understandings are both the result of physical engagement and experience in social situations and give rise to further action.

While we can differentiate cognitive emotions and emotional cognitions and physical and social actions and reactions in theory, in practice, reason and feeling and doing cannot be so easily disentangled. Between the rational and the feelingful there is a mutual dependency for emotion-free, pure rationality is impossible just as the emotions do not arise in an intellectual vacuum. Looking more widely, among the physical and rational and emotional, there is mutual dependency. But feeling can be ignored or disavowed and to that extent the potential of learning to order the world and ourselves in it is limited. It is the emotional and physical responses within learning, however, that open the possibility of admitting the sacred. It makes learning not only objectively and but also subjectively informative, encompassing both knowing and understanding, fact and meaning, doing and responding.

In what follows, we will look more closely at the particular feelings engendered by the sacred. The connection with emotion is deep and is neither inconsequential nor easily dismissed. More importantly, though the feelings may be transient or occasional, they are real and when recognized, they may occupy an important role in the experience of school and the development of understanding. Just as the joy of verification and surprise at discovering a conclusion or claim is wrong in the scientific and rational realm were the peak cognitive emotions for Scheffler, so too the sacred quest provoked by joy and surprise are the peak emotional cognitions in the sacred realm and deserve close attention. For now, we can say that harnessing the potential of joy and surprise is an invitation and challenge for teachers, curriculum designers, administrators, and all those who play a role in education.

CHAPTER 4

Feelings of the Sacred

Emotions play a significant role in knowing and being human, in learning and understanding. Nowhere is that more true than in the experience of the sacred. In fact, they are so significant in this realm that without certain feelings, there is no experience of the hallowed. We can go so far as to say that we are closer to a definition of the sacred by identifying its emotions than by any other means. We recognize the sacred especially from experience when we find ourselves saying: I don't exactly know what the sacred is, but I know it when I feel it.

Symptoms of the Sacred

In his blog, "Teaching Spirituality," Steve Habelin raises the problem of defining the related word "spirituality." In his case, he cites several writers who have identified "qualities" of spirituality, each one closely aligned with a corresponding emotion and avoids the issue of definition altogether. Among the qualities he finds in these writings notions such as aliveness, a sense of belonging, an affinity with the unknown, peace of mind, perceptions of timelessness, oneness with nature, finding God in all things, a sense of self beyond physical reality, an experience of growth and oneness, a feeling of being at home everywhere in this vast universe."[78] These qualities may be more like *products* or *results* of spiritual experience, that is, *what* becomes known and felt when we encounter the sacred. For education, this raises the questions of how this knowing is different from other kinds of knowing and how does this knowing come about.

Van der Merwe and Habron also admit the difficulty of defining spirituality (and presumably the related notion of the sacred) and point out that many writers retreat to mystical traditions that speak of its ineffability and inexpressibility and other similar qualities that defy explication. By analyzing philosophical and theoretical writings about spirituality, they sought to describe the "experience" of the spiritual. They conclude that spiritual experience is multifaceted yet integrated—incorporating corporeality, relationality, spatiality, and temporarility.[79] The explication of the encounter of the sacred by the body, in space and time, and through relationships draws attention to the wholistic nature of the experience and begins with the person himself rather than the more esoteric starting points that definitions of the sacred resort to. In their study, the selection of writers they analyze using van Manen's construction as a theoretical framework was somewhat predictive of this conclusion, but the model does provide a unique perspective on the phenomenon of spiritual experience while avoiding the morass of defining the sacred. For educators, their work also opens questions about what kind of knowledge does a sacred encounter engender and how is that knowledge expressed for clearly this kind of learning is different in fundamental ways from other kinds of knowing.

Paul Ricoeur also addresses the issue of defining the sacred. His approach is likewise phenomenological in the sense of examining how the sacred is revealed rather than being hermeneutic or interpretive within a particular tradition; he looks at what and how the sacred is manifested rather than at what is said about it. This approach is helpful because it allows an examination of the sacred outside of theology or other systems of interpretation. He draws on some of the thinkers also frequently referenced in this study, especially Rudolf Otto and Mircea Eliade. From these sources he develops a list of what he calls five "traits" of the sacred: awesomeness, "hierophany," "nonlinguisticality," revelations through the natural world, and the logic and meaning of the sacred world.[80] I discuss the first three in what follows; the latter two seem to be less like traits of the sacred and more like the means that give rise to or are a result of the former three, but his insights can go some way to unpacking what characterizes the sacred.

Nelson Goodman encountered a similar dilemma of definition in talking about art. In his book, *Languages of Art*, he describes in depth all the things that art does, but in the end, he admits to a "repeated failure to find a neat formula for sorting experiences into aesthetic and nonaesthetic." His solution was to seek a "less simple-minded approach" which would look for "aspects or symptoms, rather than a crisp criterion" of what is artistic and what is not.[81]

Symptoms, like those for an illness, are not definitive but suggestive; they are not determinative, but they may give hints, even though they may not all present themselves on all occasions. The most we can say is that there is a strong possibility that if these symptoms are present then what they point to is also likely to be present. They steer us in a likely direction. This might be a useful approach to defining the sacred since it is less determinative and absolute than Habelin's "qualities," van der Merwe and Habron's "experiences," and Ricoeur's "traits" and yet is in tune with these approaches in various ways.

It is apparent in these studies that feeling is pervasive in the encounter with the sacred and many specific emotions (such as wonder, awe, transcendence, appreciation of the self in relation to the cosmos, joy, surprise, and so on) reappear across these accounts. Here then, we can add to the understanding of the sacred by mining further the kinds of emotional symptoms the sacred evokes. This would also respond to the sense that our common understanding of the sacred is that it is something that is as much felt as it is indescribable. In the case of the sacred, the symptoms are freighted with significant affective content if they are not emotions in themselves. If that is the case, what might these feelingful symptoms be, especially in the context of schooling?

Beyond Words

The three tools in aid of sacred experiences, expressive information, passional knowledge, and imaginative reconception, based as they are in the emotional life, produce understandings that cannot necessarily be told in literal words or formulas as their counterparts can in scientific thinking. For this reason, Ricoeur suggests there is a close tie between myth (metaphorical and imaginative narratives) and the rituals that express them and the sacred for myth can better convey the meaning of the sacred than literal words.[82]

In a related vein, Howard Gardner has proposed and defended the concept of several different "frames of mind" or ways of knowing, including linguistic, musical, logical-mathematical, spatial, bodily-kinesthetic, and personal intelligences, each employing its own cognitive approach.[83] Building on his account, experiencing the sacred has much in common with both the musical intelligence, in which comprehension is intuited rather than objectively ascertained, and personal intelligence, which builds a sense of self and one's place in the world. Gardner quotes Arnold Schoenberg, who in reflecting on the work of the musician, proposes that "[t]he composer reveals the innermost essence of the world and utters the most profound vision in a language which his reason does not understand ..."[84] Like the arts and music, which are also founded in the emotional life (and incidentally have had close ties historically with experiencing and expressing the sacred), the modes of thinking about the sacred employ a different kind of language.

Suzanne Langer describes this different kind of language as one that is non-discursive. By that, she does not mean a rambling, aimless, illogical way of speaking or writing but rather "an expressive or symbolic representation of ideas that defy linguistic 'projection.'" She illustrates the difference between discursive and non-discursive languages by comparing a photograph of a painting with a verbal description of the same painting. The photograph tends to be non-discursive because there is a high correspondence between the elements of the photograph and the painting itself. On the other hand, a verbal description of the same painting does not carry that one-on-one correspondence between each word and the elements of the painting. In the painting, just the nose of the subject, for instance, is comprised of lots of colors and shades and it blends with the rest of the face: the photograph can largely reproduce this, but words cannot enumerate or capture the same multitude of nuances and details. That is a prime reason why words simply fail to do justice to it.[85]

Describing a sacred moment in words is like orally describing a painting: words simply fail to capture all the detail and the full meaning of the experience. Works of art—music, song, dance, architecture, painting, sculpture, literature, metaphor, and other non-discursive languages—may actually convey the meaning of a sacred moment more effectively than propositions made up of dictionary-defined words held together by an agreed-upon grammar.

Brendan Hyde describes a visit he made to a Grade 5 classroom where the teacher shared the Australian Aborigine Dreamtime myth about the creation of a local geographical feature, Split Rock. He saw many children in the class talking about the factual improbabilities of such an event taking place with brown snakes and a spangled drongo bird and a struggle over a hot coal. But he also heard one boy quietly pose, "It is beyond logic." Here at last was a learner who could look past the tangible world into the domain of mystery, where words and everyday logic failed. Hyde was disappointed that the teacher did not recognize the opening the boy's insight gave to discussion of a transcendent reality, a deeper meaning, and the experience of glimpsing into different kinds of space and time.[86]

In Langer's analysis, being represented in non-discursive languages does not make a moment like the sacred irrational for there is "a meaning, and therefore an element of understanding" in it.[87] Rudolf Otto, in his exploration of the sacred, agrees that such an experience is not irrational; he goes so far as to call it "supra-rational" because its essence cannot be fully captured by literal words but requires something more.[88] Understandings at this level may entail some reflection simply to identify the presence of the sacred, but once identified, it can be meaningful even if wordlessly so.

Transcendence

One of the cognitive emotions in the fullest sense of Israel Scheffler's analysis is the joy that comes from verifying a hunch or intuition. This comes about when scientific procedures are followed, facts have been objectively tested, and verifiable results established. The process carries the sense of a narrowing down, eliminating options that prove false along the way, and focusing in the end on an evidence-based conclusion. Finding that gem at the end of the process can bring a great deal of satisfaction, even joy.

The realm of the sacred does not lend itself to this kind of rational rigor as it does in the scientific mode or yield indisputable conclusions in this way. It does not carry the sense of narrowing the search for truth down to a pinpoint conclusion stated as a theorem or formula, but rather of a widening out into a whole new level or realm of understanding where the grounds of belief have moved and expanded. A specific finding in the scientific world can effect the same kind of result, and when it does, this too may be a manifestation of the sacred. A new world of meaningfulness has opened before one, broader, deeper, and more satisfying than what went before. This is the experience of transcendence.

We might metaphorically call such a breakthrough in understanding a Copernican revolution, just as the discovery that years of minute tabulations of the movement of the sun and planets confirmed, once and for all, that the earth revolved around the sun and not vice versa. Not only do we know we have found a truth, but a once-held perspective has been challenged, and we can see the world differently. And once we do that, there is no going back. We live from then on at a different plane of understanding.

Scholars of religion have long grappled with this sense of a breakthrough to a new level of meaningfulness. Eliade, for instance, frequently refers to this experience of transcendence as a breakthrough to "the really real." It is not very clear what he means by the term "the really real." He further describes the sacred as the place where one "penetrate[s] to the root of things, to ultimate reality." Again, deeply rooted knowing and ultimate reality are not particularly transparent terms but convey the sense if not the precise notion of a kind of experiential and intuitive understanding that is deeply significant and meaningful. It is helpful for the postmodern mind to see that "the really real" is not merely a kind of modernist essentialist reality but more importantly an existential reality. It is a way of being in the world rather than a way of simply knowing the world. It is, he adds, "to participate in reality, to be saturated with power,"[89] that is, it can be highly and personally consequential.

For another perspective on "ultimate reality" we can turn to the work of a contemporary of Eliade, Paul Tillich, whose project in many ways had similar goals in view and whose analysis of the sacred also took in the sweep of religious understandings across times and cultures. For Tillich, ultimate reality is the ground of being and becomes one's ultimate concern. In typical tautology, he says, "Ultimate concern is concern about the ultimate."[90] At the least, catching a sense of what is really real, beyond the poor substitutes and limitations of the immediate and transitory, is to experience, however momentarily, a concentrated and powerful focus on the ultimate or what is of greatest importance.

Eliade's conception is that the sacred is formed wherever a new construction of the world is generated that realigns the cosmos in new and more powerfully meaningful ways. Tillich's argument is that virtually anything in one's experience can serve as a symbol for this ultimate reality because it participates in it and can therefore offer a breakthrough to transcendence and add meaningfulness to existence. In other words, even everyday objects and activities can reveal the sacred. Tillich's view of this experience of the "ground of being" is mediated by encounters with powerful experiences of any kind that point to a deeper reality and addresses the questions of being and becoming.

From this account, both Eliade and Tillich picture the sacred in terms more suggestive of a quest than a destination: a search into the heart of things to find real meaning. In their respective proposals, the goal is to reach an ideal, an ultimate endpoint, but that endpoint is not readily reached, if ever. Their descriptions suggest something more akin to a calling or an invitation to embark on a journey.[91]

Their conceptions of the sacred can strike one as too remote from the teaching and learning that happens at school. "Really real" or "ultimate concern" are not expressions that find their way into statements of learning outcomes or topics outlined in a curriculum. They seem far removed from the day-to-day work of the classroom at best and unrealistically fantastic at worst. Nevertheless, they are instructive on some level. They invite us to see something simple and mundane against a larger backdrop. The lowly truths and facts and insights that come with instruction can be steps not only toward greater knowledge but toward new perspectives in personal meaning.

In other words, Eliade's really real and Tillich's ultimate reality are not of the kind that is expressed as a simple literal truth or statement of fact, the way Pythagoras' theorem or sonata form can be. Yet, when one first encounters these phenomena in a thoughtful way, the event can be a sacred moment, promoting an understanding of the world in a new and more fundamental or comprehensive way. There is a beauty and simplicity about the theorem and sonata form and the making of a palate of hues from the primary colors, and the representation of the world as sounds we call speech, and the further representation of speech as marks on a page whose mastery we call reading. When learners begin to master these fundamental skills and knowledge, shaped by their social context and personal history, their spheres of experience and perception expand. They begin to live in a world that makes more justifiable sense and are able to construct new and more comprehensive understandings of themselves and their place in it.

Seen in this light, education is a process of sequential transcendencies, each one potentially expanding the horizons of meaningfulness and understanding. This is what education is truly about; it is not about scoring well on a test or occupying a seat in a classroom for a prescribed number of years or merely preparing for a place in society with a good, wage-earning job. It may be a commonplace claim that the learner who emerges at the end of formal instruction is not the same as the person who began, and yet it is a verity through which we can view the place of the school.

Ursula Goodenough, a professor of biology, explicitly describes many topics in her field that can expose learners to a more expansive and, yes, sacred understanding of the world. She begins with the infinities and infinitesimals of nature and how the study of these opens up to the imagination the universe, its origins, and what it is made of. She talks about life, evolution, and death against this backdrop, demonstrating the sacred intuitions they evoke.[92] In doing so, she illustrates the symptom I am calling here transcendence: a study of the world and all that it is in it can engender an appreciation of what we are, where we are, and how to be. Writ large, simple learning events can be breakthroughs to transcendence, that is, breakthroughs to a more meaningful world and a deeper groundedness to living.

In recent years, "transcendence" has been juxtaposed to "immanence" for good reason. Embracing transcendence alone has focused attention on the ideal, other-worldly, even ethereal realm especially of the mind, but it has done so often at the expense of attention to this-world realities, materiality, and even physicality. It has been pointed out by women writers in particular that transcendent thinking has privileged the world of men over women who deal more personally with issues around birth, nurture, maintenance and sustenance, and death. However, while the introduction of immanence into our discourse has been a significant corrective, in the context of "whole learning," the distinction between transcendence and immanence is blurred as the two become fused in thought and deed. On the one hand, understandings gained in an experience of transcendence have direct bearing on how one should live in the here and now, while on the other hand, responding to the immediacy of living and dying, confronting a new reality, even mastering a skill can propel one into a higher, transcendent level of understanding the world and one's place in it. In human experience, there would be no transcendent insights that are not engendered by immanent reality for that is where all perceptions emerge, and no new and transcendent understandings that do not influence or inspire lived truth.

Awe

"Awesome" and the related "awful" are words that are undergoing a transition in modern usage. They are moving naturally away from their original denotation of "terror" to "wonder"[93] and maybe the even weaker "surprising" or "noteworthy" or "appealing" in informal conversation. Here, however, I am holding more closely to their historic meaning: "extremely impressive or daunting; inspiring great admiration, apprehension, or fear" and their synonyms, "breathtaking, amazing, stunning, astounding, astonishing."[94] In this usage, being awesome is both inspiring and terrifying at the same time. This comes about when we encounter something quite different, something other. It too is an emotional cognition because it is how we may feel as we begin to confront and comprehend a novel idea or phenomenon.

Again, we turn to literature in the philosophy of religion where concepts like awe have long been explored. Writing a century ago, Otto proposed and explicated the dual nature of awe. The element of fear he labeled *mysterium tremendum* where *mysterium* denotes something esoteric, beyond our full grasp, extraordinary. *Tremendum* denotes something akin to fear in the sense of dread, eeriness, uncanniness; "overpoweringness" or a feeling of dependence or self-depreciation; urgency as an energy, excitement, vitality, impetus, or force. At first glance some of these attributes of *tremendum* may seem negative but when experienced they are more like a bodily breathlessness and deep respect that accompanies an awareness of something grander and more formidable even though one is tempted to pull back from the encounter.[95]

The element of inspiration and admiration that are also a part of awe Otto called *mysterium fascinans*, indicating an attraction or fascination in contrast to fear. It is an experience of wonder, both captivating and transporting one to new heights; a yearning for more.[96] It may well be the driving force behind the quest for discovery, the appetite for learning, the need to know more or do better. Sometimes a transcendent moment may be experienced initially as the destruction of meaning rather than its expansion as old conceptions and feelings give way in shock and despair and confusion. But this can be preparation for something new.

The combination of repulsion and attraction that a learner may feel can be disquieting and lead some to argue that our teaching should not be disturbing or upsetting to students. This conception of what should and should not be taught in schools is behind the ban on certain topics in the curriculum and books in the school and public library for their capacity to trouble the mind or conscience. Such thinking, however, stultifies real learning where something different or other is encountered and the horizons of a learner's knowing are expanded. Growing pains, physical, cognitive, or emotional, can be indicators of progress and development. Without these encounters, learning can be dull and limited.

Goodenough recounts how she had "trouble with the universe." She tells of a camping trip she was on when she was a young university student. At night from her sleeping bag, she looked up at the stars that had always enchanted her. She could identify the Big Dipper and Orion. However, because of her studies in physics, she was now "overwhelmed with terror." She was so panicked, she had to bury her head and weep into her pillow. The stars she could see were part of just one galaxy among 100 billion each with their 100 billion stars. And those stars were dying, exploding, imploding, and re-fusing. This would be the destination of our sun and the planets that spun around it. It seemed all so infinitely pointless. It was an experience of *tremendum* as she glimpsed into the abyss of annihilation. But since that time, she has found an acceptance and even a *fascinans* in thinking about the universe by recognizing the ambiguity and inscrutability in that awareness. Her moment of breakthrough was to let the enormity and terror flow over her and settle into wonderment and veneration, allowing the answers to the big questions about the meaning of it all to remain unanswered as "a strange but wondrous given."[97]

Awe can be experienced across a range of intensities. It is not just an emotion of the mature thinker. The young can also be fascinated and yet fearful when learning about the different or other. In the film, *Etre et Avoir [To be and to Have]*, videographer Nicholas Philibert goes into a one-teacher schoolhouse in rural Auvergne, France with his cameras to follow the work of teacher Georges Lopez over the course of a year. Unstaged and unrehearsed, the teacher and students are captured in film as learning proceeds. At one point, Lopez is in conversation with JoJo, an irrepressible four-year-old, about how high he might be able to count.

> *How far can we count up to?*
> *A hundred.*
> *A hundred then. Are there other numbers after? ...*
> *Yes.*
> *How far?*
> *To a thousand.*
> *Can you go further than a thousand? 1001, 1002 ...?*
> *1003 ...*
> *How far can we go after that? Can we keep on counting?*
> *No.*
> *Without stopping?*
> *(Grunt from JoJo.)*
> *Can we say 2000? 3000?*
> *3000, 4000 ...*

10,000? …
30,000 …
After 90,000?
100,000!
We have to stop there? …
One billion …
Can you say 12 billion? …
It's like when you pay with notes.
With notes? Do you have a lot of notes in your piggy bank?
Only 2 …
Can you go beyond billions?
Sir, look at all the animals. (They were in a library looking at books.)
Yes, they're nice. Can you go beyond billions?
No!
You told me you could count forever. (JoJo looks around.) Can we go on counting?

By gently questioning and urging JoJo to consider the next possibilities it gradually becomes apparent to the young learner that there seems to be no end to numbers. JoJo begins to look for distractions and to squirm. He directs attention to another pupil who seems to be crying. This may be simply because he is a child of high action and low attention, but one wonders too if his squirming at this moment is also an indication that he knows he is on the cusp of some new wonder about numeration. The enormity of his first glimpse into infinity appears to make him shrink from this new idea. Even if the full realization of what he has now learned is not appreciated by JoJo, one thing is likely: his world after this episode is ever so slightly different from the world he knew before; he has stepped into a new dimension of experience, he has transcended the ordinary and glimpsed the extraordinary. He, like all learners, was for that moment on holy ground.

Awe is not an everyday emotion; it is a peak experience that comes at a dramatic moment and lingers in the memory. There are, however, many other emotions that relate to awe and may even prepare the way for an awesome experience or follow it as an aftereffect. One thinks, for instance, of anticipation and excitement. Something wonderful is about to happen; maybe it is an updated computer with added features, a new library privilege, an upcoming excursion, a classroom visitor, or for the older student, a new lead in pursuing a research question or admission to a course that holds promise for their professional development. Curiosity may drive one toward finding an awesome resolution. Then too are the emotions of satisfaction and a sense of accomplishment, a sense of finding all the parts fit together after being awed. A project has been completed, a written account edited so that it sings, a move on the sports field masterfully undertaken, a play performed to audience applause, a math problem solved. Inspiration to think and do and be differently can follow. Capturing these preliminary and ensuing emotions, ordinary though they may be, can open the learner to extraordinary and even awesome possibilities.

Surprise

Among the descriptions of the cognitive emotions, Scheffler included surprise. This comes about, he explains, when an anticipated conclusion proves to be wrong. This kind of surprise is the shock of recognition that what one held as true turns out to be false. It can prove to be a stimulus to seek an alternative path to a better conclusion. Surprise is also a symptom of the sacred, that comes from an encounter with unexpectedness and unpredictability. It occurs not so much as seeking for truth but of truth suddenly coming to one. This can happen whether one is solving a mathematical problem, testing a scientific hypothesis, composing a song, building an argument, or designing the plot for a short story. The path forward is suddenly there.

In teaching my college-level service-learning course, we made a connection between the topics and issues we covered in class and the students' involvement working in the local homeless shelter. There were many occasions when shock and surprise were experienced by us all, as we listened to the stories of the unhoused, their frustrations, failures, hopes. One incredible story we heard was told by a woman from the shelter and my co-teacher who volunteered at the shelter. The child welfare department had removed the woman's children from her care when her life spun out of control, and she was living on the streets. She was discovered one day in the university's law library poring over reference books. A couple of the students challenged her, and she admitted to them she was trying to find a legal way to get her children back with her. They were stirred by her plight and while admitting they had no qualification to help her legally, they could at least bookmark for her the places in the books where she might find a pathway forward. When she visited my class, she announced she had used the procedures she discovered and had already won back custody of two of her children. Her excitement was palpable and moving. Then she announced that if she could get her General Education Certificate (GED), she would be eligible to apply for a job and qualify to have her third child returned. Would anybody in the class be willing to tutor her? One of the students nearly leaped out of her seat. She would be more than willing. They were to meet on a specified day and time at the public library for the first session. My student arrived on time and waited, but the woman did not appear. Another date and time were set, and another, but she did not turn up. Back in class, the student broke down. Angry and tearful she was frustrated and almost speechless. She was deeply shocked that her would-be learner, with so much at stake and having gone so far, would let this opportunity slip through her fingers. My co-teacher who was familiar with the woman gently explained that working with the people at the shelter was filled with disappointments like this because recidivism rates were high, but even knowing this, we must still work with and for them. I do not know what became of the woman and her children, but I do know that a couple of years later, I heard from the student who had been so shocked and frustrated. She called me to tell me that she was working with the State Division of Family Resources because of that experience in class. The surprise and unpredictability of that encounter with the homeless mother had opened a career path for her. She saw those families in need in a new light, it was a turning point for her, and she wanted to commit to working with them for a better life.[98]

Religions have used the word "epiphany" to describe these ah-ha moments in a faith journey. Eliade preferred *hierophany* from the ancient Greek, where *hieros* designates the sacred and *phainô*, to show or appear, because it suggests "something sacred shows itself." It might be manifested through an ordinary object like a stone or a tree, he suggests, or something "of a wholly different order," even "mysterious." He interprets these experiences in religious terms, but at the least they are moments when the ordinary, profane world is seen as extraordinary and sacred.[99] It is akin to seeing things differently, creating the world anew, and it can be "generated on whatever scale."[100]

Hierophany suggests the experience of the sacred at times is not initiated by a deliberate action on the part of the learner or instigated by the teacher. It comes unexpectedly and surprisingly. That does not mean, however, that we are forced to wait on surprise. When teaching is more than the presentation of facts and learning is more than absorbing these facts to be repeated back when called on, that is, when knowledge and skill are opened to reflection and acted on, then the unexpected can happen.

* * *

When learners encounter a new idea or see something beyond the immediate realities of the information they are tackling in their studies, they may well be experiencing the hallowed. Here they may find themselves at a loss for words when expressing what is felt or newly intuited because words fail to capture the fullness of the moment. It is an experience of stepping from where former views of who they are and what they know are transcended and widen to a broader and deeper realm of understanding. It embraces moments of awe and breathtaking wonder, maybe even a fearful sense of being on the cusp of really knowing something in a way not contemplated before. It is acknowledging and accepting the shock and surprise of an unexpected and novel way of seeing the world and all that is in it. If these moments of heightened feeling occur at times in the course of study, over time and naturally, the learning is likely to be sacred and powerful.

Calling attention to the symptoms of the sacred suggested here has not resorted to mysticism or the mystery traditions. They are not other-worldly and esoteric. Each of the symptoms are embedded in human experience: they invoke both sense and sensation, real feelings, bodily impressions, greater awareness, deeper insight, and a growing understanding. In the context of education, they can be life-changing and provoke response and action and wisdom.

Whenever learning manifests these symptoms, then the school is functioning as sacred. We turn now to look at the particularities of the school as sacred: the possibilities captured in the concepts of "lived space," "lived time,"[101] and lived ritual.

CHAPTER 5

Sacred Place

The town hall, the bank, the supermarket, the church, the hospital, the funeral home, the park, the garage, the pizza parlor, your home, and the school are places we might experience frequently, but each place will likely be experienced differently. While we may measure the length and breadth of a space, determine its area and topography, and locate it on a map, each one can also be encountered differently and engender different feelings that cannot necessarily be quantitively determined. This is not only because they serve different purposes, but our personal histories have been built around and in them. Whether our experiences in a place have given rise to awe or anger, hope or despair, love and the comforting familiar or disdain and contempt, those experiences will color our attitude to that place, even subconsciously, as the places we frequent color our behavior and feelings toward them. In Max van Manen's account, spatiality is another "lifeworld existential." It is one of the ways "human beings experience the world;" "it is felt space" and, as such, has more to do with how one lives in different spaces than it has to do with distance or geography.[102]

Space is the setting that builds in us a sense of who we are psychologically, cognitively, socially, physically, and morally, for good or bad, as we interact with ideas, family, teachers, friends, and other people, events, and ethical dilemmas. Being submerged in the immanence and intimacy of a space can evoke an intuition of the transcendent, opening up a glimpse into what is "really real"[103] or of "ultimate concern,"[104] and that in turn can provoke a moral response or physical action. Leisl van der Merwe and John Habron propose that "awareness, awe and wonder, transcendence, ecstasies, and suprarationality" are potential "categories" of lived space.[105] In an important sense, then, appreciating space in qualitative terms opens the possibility that some places can be experienced as sacred.

Sacred space is different and special, distinguishable from the other spaces around it. It is a walled off place in our minds to be protected, cherished, and cultivated. Within that space, participants can be transformed; they can transcend the ordinary and reach toward the extraordinary. The school or wherever learning happens can be such a place.

In his summary of sacred space as recorded in his *Patterns of Comparative Religion*, Mircea Eliade describes the following recurring themes. Such a space is first of all where creation and new life begin, acting as a kind of "navel," or "embryo," a point of origin from which the world spreads out in different directions.[106] It is also a center, a meeting place of earth and heaven, and a replica of the cosmos.[107] Entry into such a space is by initiates and may be fraught with obstacles and, therefore, getting inside is meritorious. Paradoxically, it is also accessible.[108] The ambivalence of sacred space is further manifested in that it both "attracts and repels, is useful and dangerous, brings death as well as immortality."[109] It is a place constructed by myth and any sacred space is the repetition of an archetype or symbol that "reveals to us something about [our] place in the cosmos."[110] And an experience of sacred space generates a "nostalgia for paradise."[111]

Contemporary indigenous peoples have not lost this sense of sacred space despite colonial takeovers and displacement from their ancestral homes. Native Australians (the aboriginal peoples),[112] Native Americans,[113] the Sami people who live above the Arctic Circle,[114] and other indigenous peoples around the world remind us as forcefully as they can that for them the land and its distinctive features are sacred and hold the promise of identity and fulfillment for them.

One might say at this point that the qualities of sacred space for archaic and some contemporary peoples may be just like Eliade has described them, but they may seem a long way from the reality of a room full of squirming children, moody or distracted adolescents, or overextended, anxious young adult learners. If, however, the symbolic power of the school today bears some resemblance, even figuratively, to ancient beliefs about the sacred, then the school could rightfully be regarded as a sacred space.

Clearly, school, like archetypical sacred spaces described by Eliade, does open new levels of understanding life and living it more effectively. What is learned during the school years spreads out from the classroom through the life of the learner and to the community that the learner occupies. In that way, school becomes a center or grounding for the life that will be lived and when it embodies the values of the community, it replicates the best of the community. John Dewey, for instance, argued that "each one of our schools" should be conducted as an "embryonic community life" along the lines of society's ideals for itself. In doing so, the school would have "the deepest and best guaranty of a larger society which is worthy, lovely, and harmonious."[115]

Entry into school is not the same as entry into most other places. It requires a degree of severance from the comforts of familiar life up to that point, whether it is stepping off the bus at school on the first day or leaving home for a college residence hall or confronting new and disruptive ideas. Sometimes entry is difficult and has to be earned by the learner's diligent effort. No matter how appealing going to school might be, there is always the fear of not being accepted by others, not making the team, keeping up with others, choosing the most appropriate school or major, exploring one's sexuality, or passing examinations. When they complete the course and graduate, many will look back on their good old school days with nostalgia expressed, for instance, in class reunions or *home*comings.

In these ways, we can look at the school through the lens of sacred space as described by Eliade, going beyond the ordinary and mundane. If that is our basic starting point, we can indeed imagine and maybe even recognize moments when the world opened wider to inquiring minds, when something happened surprisingly and beyond words in how learners see themselves anew and their place in the world, when they balance on the cusp of a new understanding, or when they light up as a new understanding breaks through. It can happen when they connect with a friend or the teacher or when they achieve a new academic goal or personal best in some undertaking. It is also evident when a new beginning or change of direction is made, as for instance, when a learner settles on something as life-changing as a career choice, makes a discovery that opens up new paths for exploration, or is newly motivated to apply herself to solving a current problem, embarks on a new project, chooses a different major, picks up a new skill to master, or begins a new term with gusto. These occasions may not all seem momentous at the time, but in the course of a life, they may be highly significant. And even if they are brief and passing, recognizing them and naming them as sacred can capture their significance in the larger view. In essence, sometimes it is not only *what* we see but *how* we see it that makes it meaningful. And sacred. Above all, we have in Eliade's descriptions of literal sacred places and the power of these places a metaphor for what occurs in the learning environment. Through the mind's eye we can recognize and interpret places of importance and be encouraged to plan for them to be entered and occupied with an awareness of the potential of being there.

Learning in Sacred Space

The dictum, "Form follows function," intimates that the reason for a space, the role it is meant to fulfill, should determine the very shape and look of the space. For our purposes here, that means that how one intends to conduct teaching and learning should be reflected in the sense of the place where that educational process happens. We can illustrate this with contrasting scenarios.

The first is fictional. "The scene was a plain, bare, monotonous vault of a schoolroom ..." In his satire, *Hard Times*, Charles Dickens paints the scene of an egregious education experience, ruled over by a Mr. Thomas Gradgrind, the schoolmaster, who was no more appealing than the school building itself. He had a "square forefinger" to stab toward those he called on. He had a "square wall of a forehead, which had eyebrows for its base, while his eyes found commodious cellarage in the dark caves overshadowed by the wall." His mouth was "wide, dry, and hard set"; his voice "inflexible, dry, dictatorial"; his hair "bristled"; his carriage was "obstinate;" his coat was "square" as were his legs and shoulders.[116]

The school space and the headmaster were perfectly matched. And so was the educational philosophy practiced in that setting. They were all of a kind. "[T]he spring of the mechanical art and mystery of educating," Gradgrind proclaimed, was to "not stoop to cultivate the sentiments and affections. Never wonder!"[117] Instead, he lorded it over "the inclined plane of little vessels then and there arranged in order, ready to have imperial gallons of facts poured into them until they were full to the brim." He was "a man of facts and calculations ... with a rule and a pair of scales and the multiplication table always in his pocket ... ready to weigh and measure any parcel of human nature and tell you exactly what it comes to." He "seemed a kind of cannon loaded to the muzzle with facts and prepared to blow [his pupils] clean out of the regions of childhood at one discharge.... charged with a grim mechanical substitute for the tender young imaginations that were to be stormed away."[118] "[T]hou wilt always kill outright the rabble Fancy lurking within!"[119] In this school, children were bullied, pitted against one another, and wrapped in fear of the school master. As the story unfolds, we see how ineffective and even disastrous this education proved to be for pupils Sissy and Blitzer and the Gradgrind children. Such a school can hardly be called a sacred space, a hallowed hall of learning.

While the scene may be overdrawn for satirical purposes, such an approach to education and its rigid setting casts a long shadow. In his review of Jane Roland Martin's *School Was Our Life*, Randall Allsup contrasts the joyous learning in the Little Red School House of Martin's childhood with what he sees today out of his window overlooking an elementary charter school in Harlem, NY. High stakes testing and teaching to the test make this school a standout as a high achiever in the neighborhood. But Allsup sees another side. During recess, which is when he can really observe what is happening, the children file out to the playground "in strict lines determined by height." There is no touching while at play and infractions are called out by the sounding of a very loud whistle. Everybody freezes in place until the "offender is sentenced and removed." These infractions seem to occur among the 40 or so children every couple of minutes, so play has to be conducted in two minute intervals until the students are formed again into lines and marched back into the building. Allsup does not ask "how things got this way," but rather "why can't we see that this way of schooling is so terribly wrong?"[120]

An alternative scenario is real and has been very influential. Maria Montessori had a different philosophy of education from that of the fictional Mr. Gradgrind or the actual charter school in NY, and she practiced it in a very different setting. She was born the year Dickens died (1870) and like him focused on the marginalized children of the new industrial age. Her school room was filled with color, manipulatives, activity corners, story books, movement, and discovery. She led her charges as individuals, prompting them forward with questions, but never forcing them to give back the right answers until they were ready and able. There was no "blowing children out their childhood," for she advocated age-appropriate learning which took into account the changing developmental needs and capacities of learners from childhood through adolescence and beyond, always with the goal of having them "move from one stage of independence to a higher, by means of their own activity, through their own effort of will, which constitutes the inner evolution of the individual."[121] In the classroom of the youngest pupils, the desks were light and movable rather than heavy, fixed, and therefore trapping children into a fixed and rigid position. Everyone could move about freely and had to show care and reverence in the schoolroom space.[122] She did not rely on a reward system or promote competition among her learners but cultivated their intrinsic motivation and found that cooperation among them came quite naturally in this setting.[123]

Montessori stood in a line of teachers and educational philosophers who understood that authentic learning in large part would be learning-by-doing rather than learning-by-rote. And such an education would require its own kind of space. Even today, schools that are not strictly speaking Montessorian will have light, movable desks that can be arranged in different configurations, activity corners, a place for stories or movement, music, color, and light. Designed to be age-appropriate and hospitable, such learning spaces exhibit the symptoms of the sacred: they allow for learning to engender wonder, draw the learners into new dimensions of understanding themselves and the world around them, they build community, and enable the joy of discovery.

In *School Was Our Life* to which Allsup was responding above, Martin and her fellow students recall their early years as students in the Little Red School House in Greenwich Village, NY, during the Depression and in the early years of the World War II. "Little Red," as the school was fondly known, had such a powerful effect on shaping the lives of its attendees, that over six decades later, Martin and many of her fellow classmates would still regard themselves as the "Lucky Ones" for having been students there.[124] The school was a simple three-story building to which was added a four story high school named after the founder of Little Red, Elisabeth Irwin. The very name of the school, the Little Red School House, is evocative, conjuring the image of a colorful, welcoming home for a community of learners, even though the actual buildings had quite plain and predictable facades, and there was nothing about them that was either red or "cottagy." It had a piano, a printing press, and other materials for team projects (learners at one point actually learned how to wrap a mummy and at another time built a two-story pueblo out of beams and cardboard as a class assignment[125]). They were actively involved in spelling bees, poetry writing, singing, and composing. Teachers were free to recognize and use unplanned events as teaching moments and create opportunities for learners who were failing to succeed at something else. The principal's office was like a library, full of books with a couch, and it was a pleasure to be sent there. At one point, when the autoworkers went on strike, the students indicated they too would like to go on strike. They had a sparse list of demands, perhaps just a complaint about their mandated rest time, but one of the teachers suggested they needed a room to meet secretly and a committee to lead them. The students, as a result, had the experience of being on strike, which is all they really wanted anyway.[126] "Shame, wrath, and pugnacity" had no place, and no grades, prizes, awards, dunce caps, or gold stars were used as incentives.[127] As adults reflecting on their experience at Little Red, the former students reported that as children they felt safe and cared for, they loved school, they did not look on their school work as drudgery for play and work merged in their experience. With an open and flexible curriculum, team projects, plays, creative writing, reenactments, summer camps, and excursions were occasions for "knowledge by acquaintance;"—wholistic learning, where teachers "inscribed academic learning on bodies, minds, emotions, and their selves."[128] The learning environment focused on social interaction: the assemblies established a common culture, classes stayed together from year to year, learners always sat in a circle, and the physical arrangements of the school pointed toward community. The school's mission, restated in 2014, sums up the history of the school: "A leader in progressive education since 1921, [Little Red School House] teaches children to be independent thinkers who work together to solve complex problems." Further, "Students graduate from our diverse community as active participants in our democratic society, with the creativity, integrity, and courage to bring meaningful change to the world." It has always been "an exciting place to learn, with a palpable spirit of curiosity, creativity and challenge."[129]

Martin doubts "that any single model of school can fit all children." We live in a different world now, but she writes "in the belief that we can learn from the best schools" (charter, public private, parochial, independent) and "also from the best progressive schools of this nation's past."[130] Given the nature of the curriculum and serendipitous lines of inquiry that opened as opportunity allowed, the learners "might have missed a little bit of information or technique," but they gained instead "sound and wholesome habits of thinking and of acting."[131]

The underlying principles that guide the design of classrooms for the very young have been applied equally to all levels of schooling,[132] with special purpose rooms, studios, laboratories, seminar rooms, and lounges. And in some cases, rather than "blowing" learners out of their developmental level, the classroom itself has been blown out of its four walls. From the experimental thinking of Rousseau and Pestalozzi, educators have accepted that all learning need not be conducted within four walls at all. The "open classroom" became in some instances "schools without walls" and even "universities without walls" as learners took their questions and research into workplaces and other community settings off-campus. Mentors and their graduate students have gathered around kitchen tables and other off-site locations near the workplace and the issues their research was addressing.[133] When form follows function, and if the function is to empower learners and create an environment where learning is productive and meaningful, teachers and learners are on sacred ground.

Architecture

The layout and structural elements of sacred places are not always designed with considerations of function alone, however. A great deal of attention is given to symbolic elements as well. The still reflecting pools of water and the rich mosaics in many mosques and temples speak of tranquility and refreshment in contrast to their hot and dusty surroundings; the single minaret is a proclamation of an aggressive and total monotheism. The architectural footprint in the shape of a cross and the high domed ceilings, tall stained-glass windows, and spires directing the eye and the mind upwards capture Christian theology sometimes more powerfully than words can. And the ziggurats, groves, mountains, rocks, and rivers of other faiths indicate not only sacred places but express sacred meanings as well.[134]

So, what of the architecture of our places of learning? This presents a mixed picture. At a large state university where I spent several years advising an academic program for undergraduates, there were two kinds of residence hall: the stripped down, cement block, impersonal stretches of hallways of closed doors and student-proof fixtures, and alternatively, the limestone clad, wood paneled, flexible common areas, and classic lines of an earlier era that spoke of respect for learning and learners. The first buildings were often the sites of rowdiness and "party animals"; the others were home to book clubs, drama productions, poetry readings, debates, music, and art. I do not believe that the different architectural styles *caused* the different lifestyles, but I do suspect they worked together in some way. Again, in our planning spaces for learning, form should follow function; that is, we design the space to give shape to our philosophy of education. Paradoxically, function can also follow form, when the seat of learning, its buildings and rooms, corridors and windows, entryways and furniture arrangements presume or even impose a way of being in that space.

In the US, the architecture and upkeep of schools is largely financed by local property taxes, so in effect, wealthy neighborhoods generally build commodious, well-appointed schools and poor neighborhoods do the best they can, with sometimes alarming differences between the two. There is a direct link between what a community actually pays in taxes and what the children in that community experience as a school facility and yet there is also growing resistance and inability in some school districts to property tax rates proposed to keep up with growing enrollments and aging buildings, asbestos in the walls, and unreliable heating, cooling, clean air, and plumbing.[135]

Of course, where resources are justifiably in short supply and the school cannot afford fine architecture and building supplies, deficiencies can be made up somewhat if the community attends to the school thoughtfully. I once visited a primary school in a small village on the South Pacific island Kingdom of Tonga. While I was inside meeting with teachers and pupils, the mothers were sitting outside on the grass under palm trees, waiting and watching for my reaction when I emerged. There it did not seem to matter that the concrete steps had begun to drift away from the building itself, that tapa cloth was all that divided one room from another, that there were more children than desk seats, and that there were no textbooks at all. The school was centrally located, built on stilts so that it rose taller than all the other buildings in the village, and it was the pride and joy of all. As I left, the mothers presented me with the "first fruits" from the school garden—some sticks of sugar cane, a coconut, and a beautifully woven basket—as a solemn parting gift. I thought how rich those children really were to be in such a space dedicated to their learning and loved and supported by the villagers. Again, paradoxically, while we may build walls of protection around learning spaces to keep threats and danger away from learners, we would also want those borders to be "soft boundaries"[136] that allow support and care, engagement and devotion, pride and pleasure to flow from the community to infuse the school setting.

By contrast, some years later, my class of teachers-in-training took an excursion to get acquainted better with inner-city schools. One group reported back that when the bus dropped them off in a cul-de-sac, they could not tell which building was the school, for all around were barred and boarded windows, crumbling masonry, shattered glass, and general urban blight. The architecture here, at least what was left of the original, did not give any sense of specialness to the students or the learning their teachers would try to encourage behind those boarded windows and broken walls.

No one in the community seemed to or, sadly and more likely, was able to care about the school.

There is no single architectural style to convey the notion that the school is set aside as a sacred space; rather, this is something that needs to be determined school by school, depending on the context and mission of the institution. A flight of ascending stairs, a tall roof, windows bearing student work and letting in maximum light, and large open doors are common elements speaking of the lofty ideals of the school and the welcome that students will receive when they enter, while re-purposed huts and large sprawling factory-like buildings draw on different metaphors and convey other and often unfortunate messages. When Quonset huts were erected to cope with the explosion of baby boomers entering school in the 1950s, even those unimposing buildings could testify to the value the community placed on education—they were there despite building shortages and overwhelming demands. Even in the worst of conditions teachers can work to create a welcoming, disciplined, and aspirational place for learning and becoming by adding decorative features, how they arrange the seating, what is chosen for display, and how they expect the space to be treated. The deciding factor is the lived experience in the space that is set aside for learning.

Centers and Boundaries

A feature of sacred space is that it is clearly differentiated from the surrounding secular, chaotic space by a distinct boundary. Eliade records a variety of perimeters that have served this purpose from a ring of stones or a simple enclosure to the massive walls and buttresses of the great cathedrals. The enclosed area is treated as existentially different from the surrounding area and the demeanor of participants changes when they enter. It is no surprise, given this sense of boundedness and sacrality, that temples, churches, and mosques have served as places of refuge both literally and figuratively for people seeking relief. To breach such a space is a double crime: one against those who call it sacred and the other against the very notion of sacred space itself. The enclosure of such a space is supposed to be protective and the space a safe place. The school boundary is breached when disturbed people with guns in their hands break in, or angry parents storm a school board meeting, or partisans demand a curriculum that complies with their personal ideology, or teachers are disempowered in governing the conditions of their employment, or their freedoms as teachers and researchers are circumscribed.

For many children, going to school amounts to entering a center of protection and predictability in a chaotic and dangerous world, psychologically and sometimes physically. In settings of violence on the streets and instability in the home, school can be a sanctuary, a sacred space. But even for children from happy homes and well-ordered neighborhoods, attending school for learning, the development of life skills, and the formation of long-term relationships with peers and teachers can be understood as attending to a sacred center.

For all children, school should be experienced as a safe place for trying out new ideas and finding one's own voice and beliefs. When schools fulfill this role as sacred place in the heart of society, the community, whether it is strife ridden or congenial for its people, can draw on and extend the qualities of security and harmony for free thought beyond the boundaries of the schoolyard.

Most schools are enclosed spaces literally and metaphorically. Students know when they are in bounds or out of bounds. Sometimes the perimeter is marked by a chain-link fence and in the United States by ciphers such as the Safe Place sign with its encircling arms symbol or the Drug Free Zone sign. Teachers assume "yard duty" within their bounded space. The school staff and administrators are very serious about protecting the children in their care from predatory others, hostile parents, and natural or man-made disasters once the children have entered the school grounds. Because of threats of violence, many school buildings have to be protected by guarded entries or security barriers. Some schools require their students to pass through metal detectors on their way inside. Other protections lie in the Right to Privacy act that prohibits non-authorized people, including parents of college age young people, from viewing student records that give contact information and even grade reports.

Another bounded space that carries a similar gloss of the sacred is the home and intersections of the two spaces, the home and the school, have been explored by several writers, at least as far back as Montessori, with her founding of the *Casa dei Bambini* (children's houses).[137] Building on Montessori's work, Martin, in *The Schoolhome*, has argued that the school needs to fill the vacuum created by parents absent for one reason or another; that the school should be "a big hug" for children, meeting their cognitive, social, physical, and psychological needs.[138] In *Starting at Home*, Nel Noddings extrapolates from the ideal home guidelines of caring by which the school and the larger society should govern their respective charges.[139] These insights contribute to a richer understanding of both home and school by bringing the two institutions into closer alignment with and in support of each other.

The metaphor of the home has also been ascribed to the content or subject matter of the curriculum. It too can be seen as a space to be occupied—a field of study, an area of expertise, a home to be occupied. Albi Odendaal describes the home as a place with many rooms, some where one feels more at home but others that also beckon. In music education, he elaborates, the music one is most comfortable and familiar with occupies the living room; music of other genres and cultures might be found in other rooms. Venturing beyond what is predictable and feels safe is a step to widening understanding, even though these other rooms may seem forbidding at first.[140] Odendaal's image illuminates an education that is deliberately risk-taking and daring in its willingness to open learners to new vistas and one that also promotes their growth in and appreciation of their world, yet like the home, still conducted in a secure boundaried environment.

Understanding the school in terms of sacred space, however, provides a dimension that the home metaphor characteristically does not. The home is the place for significant, ongoing, but more informal learning that usually occurs as occasions allow. And much of the learning comes about by modeling, "dinner table" discussions, and experiences planned or unplanned that are part of family life. The home touches our emotional selves deeply and these emotions and the sense of self they engender are a part of us for the rest of our lives. School, on the other hand, has its curriculum and is charged with offering formal and systematic learning opportunities. It too comes with an emotional impact from our association with teachers, other learners, and the world of knowledge itself. At times, learning may even evoke a sense of *mysterium tremendum*, a sense of "something uncanny, eerie, or weird" that may become more akin to fear, dread, and ultimately awe.[141] This may be accompanied by *mysterium fascinans*, an amalgamation of wonder, captivation, entrancement, bewilderment, even "dizzying intoxication."[142] Such emotional responses should be part of the experience of the school because ideas, understandings, insights, and knowledge are sacred for their power to fill us and our learners with awe and wonder and personal effectiveness.

Thresholds

Thresholds are another important element in sacred space, marking the very place where the profane gives way to the sacred. They are where transformation into the sacred begins.

The prominence of the threshold seems to be the consistent design element across sacred spaces although they vary from culture to culture and across time. In Greece, for instance, many chapels are entered through a very low door which opens immediately onto a set of stairs going down into the sanctuary. Bending low and navigating the stairs takes some focus. In many Buddhist temples, one must not only take off one's shoes before entering but also step over a substantial doorstep. In India, Diana Eck tells how she wound her way into the heart of a temple toward a massive reclining figure of Vishnu, through a dark and spiraling labyrinth, accompanied by an oil lamp which cast a golden moving glow, the sound of beating drums, clanging bells, and whining reed instruments.[143] Many cathedrals are approached through a long and wide flight of stairs. One way to access an open-air classroom of monks in Lhasa, Tibet requires the visitor to climb a steep stairway with very narrow treads, almost forcing the visitor to enter on hands and knees. All of these entryways into sacred space are built to slow down participants and visitors, demanding that they step carefully, and be aware of where they are, compelling them to realize that they are leaving the profane and ordinary and entering the sacred and extraordinary.

In some way, perhaps by the presence of a teacher, or the design of the doorway, or the pathway to that doorway, the entry into the school should be marked and clear. And just as religious peoples have removed their shoes, or donned headscarves, or dipped their fingers into a bowl of sacred water, or attached a mezuzah to the lintel, the deportment of the students and their teachers should change once the school space is entered to signify that the activities of learning and the sacred tasks of the school are about to begin in earnest. Rituals of waiting for the teacher in a preordained area, lining up outside the classroom, or gathering for the pledge of allegiance help to mark the threshold of the place and the time for learning.

The idea of "the school gate" has become a signifier in legal talk about schools, for some things change once the teacher and student step through that portal. In the US, for instance, teachers assume the role of *in loco parentis* once their students enter the school grounds and assume the heavy responsibility of acting as parents would on behalf of their children.

Marking the threshold to expose its significance as the entry into the school becomes more challenging when learning does not take place in a bricks and mortar building. More and more, schools are offering courses and whole programs online, a development that got an extra boost during the 2019–22 COVID-19 pandemic. Now that the platforms for online learning have been established, meeting in classrooms for instruction is readily replaced during a storm or other emergency and is often used to supplement work done in class. Yet even in this context, there is an entry point, a sign-in page, pointedly called a "portal." Rather than showing a list of instructions for how to navigate the lesson or even laying out the first assignment as soon as the learner logs in, the portal can do much more by serving as an open welcome and a shared excitement for what the class members are about to do. It can provide an overview of the course putting it into context and highlighting its value to the learner. It will make links to the help desk and the instructor easy to find. It may also find a way for students to introduce themselves and get to know their classmates in a more personal way. From there, finding occasions at the beginning of lessons or courses of study to reiterate the meaningfulness of their entry into this learning experience helped focus attention and motivate effort. In my experience teaching for some time in an online university, I saw that students moved into the program more successfully and smoothly if we could spend some face-to-face time with them first, acting as an entryway, giving them a sense of the mission and values that shape the curriculum and an opportunity to connect them with professors and fellow learners.

A precursor to online learning was the correspondence school. This was helpful for learners unable to attend a school or university. The children on the far-flung stations (ranches) of the Australian outback belonged to such a group. Lessons and learning aids arrived by mail. But even for them, the teachers realized there was a need for something more that would bring the children into a learning mode, motivated and ready to get to work on their studies. To do this, the children were connected to their teachers and other learners through the School of the Air. The school day would begin with children calling in on their shortwave radios. The session would open with a roll call and if a child could not be reached by the teacher because of atmospheric conditions, his classmates would try from their locations. When everyone was in, the teacher would chat with them, there would be a time to share what was happening on their stations, and sometimes they would even sing together before going to their own individual assignments for the day, altogether and a much-loved entryway to learning. If any school is going to be experienced as a sacred space, then consideration of the threshold becomes important.

The threshold or *limen* is also a metaphor for a transitional point in one's experience, both a psychological and physiological entryway to a new status. It is a transition point between the ordinary and the extraordinary. And it is a place that can begin a transformation of self-understanding, wisdom, and meaning.

The arts are particularly potent in creating this liminal space. In music, for example, June Boyce-Tillman, quoting Lori Custodero, describes how the elements of a piece of music—the actual tones, rhythms, and musical lines—become an aesthetic experience, transporting the listener beyond the mere sounds.[144] A work of visual art—painting, sculpture, or architecture—calls the viewer to sense a meaning beyond the materials that make up the work, evoking interest and attention and possibly a sense of awe and wonder. Literature in the form of plays, novels, poetry, or biographies, or cast as movies, creates different times and places, inviting the reader to enter through them into another place and time and experience their meaning. An encounter with a natural phenomenon—a star-filled sky, a snowy peak reflected in a mirror-like lake, a stunning sunset, a field of sunflowers, or an up-close view of a bumblebee—can also be a *limen*. These entry points can only become liminal, Boyce-Tillman reminds us, when we actually *encounter* the work. One's past history or value-system or reticence to engage otherness may hold one back from the threshold and alert teachers to the need to prepare their learners for what is possible. Among the qualities of liminal space, Boyce-Tillman rephrases many of the symptoms of the sacred when she lists among them "a paradoxical knowing," "a sense of empowerment," "a sense of the beyond," "a feeling of an opening-up in the experiencer," and "an evanescent and fleeting quality that cannot be controlled."[145] However the place is described in mere words, it serves as a transition point to discovery and deeper meaning.

Inner Sancta

As sacred space is centered in the midst of chaos and secularity, within it is a most sacred center, the inner sanctum. It may be marked by an altar or icon, or tallest tree in the sacred grove. While the whole space may be carefully tended, special attention is paid to the rituals that take place and the mysteries that are encountered in this sacred center, and often only the initiate is permitted to enter and participate. Whatever significance and meaning the sacred space might have, it is intensified here.

Schools too may have an inner sanctum. For some, the sacred space is one's own carrel in the library among the books and journals; for others, it is being with the beakers and Bunsen burners of the science lab, or the music studio with its array of instruments, or the bats, balls, and padding of the sports field, or the comfortableness and familiarity of the homeroom, or maybe the principal's office. For younger learners it may be wherever the teacher happens to be; while for the college student it may be the coffee lounge where ideas are proposed and worked over with co-learners. Each place can be a bearer of intensified feelings and power.

At a high school where I once taught, there was a small quadrangle with a tall brick wall at one end. The tarmac was marked with painted lines. In that space the daily ritual of "bat tennis" took place. The game was simple enough: hitting the ball in turn against the wall and within the lines drawn on the pavement all governed by strict rules negotiated over time. The students had constructed bats to their liking with the boys usually doing the construction according to prescribed dimensions and the girls the decorations. Teams were drawn up and every recess saw a stampede down to the space. The players knew every crack and bump in the pavement that could be used to their advantage.

The court was more than a play area. It was where students learned to form deep friendships, acquire the skills of teamwork, accept differences among the players, enjoy exercising in the outdoors, and develop healthy attitudes about having fun, winning, and losing. The day came, sadly, when the school was to be renovated and the big brick wall was torn down. Even more sadly, little progress in the renovation took place for months and an equivalent wall was never in the plans. The students would look at the demolished court with grief and resentment. When one of their number passed away decades later, her former classmates brought bats and balls to her memorial service and held an impromptu game to celebrate her life. These many years later, those students were still chagrined at the loss of their court but cherished the memories of their time there. To them, this space had always been an inner sanctum.

Choosing even subliminally a learner's inner sanctum cannot always be prescribed. The bat-tennis highschoolers found theirs just as other learners may find theirs in lab or library or homeroom. Permission to enter into that space may be selective and a different and probably stricter code of conduct may govern behavior while being there. Teachers may not always be the most appropriate deciders on these issues, but they can enable and guide learners in establishing their center of activity and meaning. To recognize the strong commitments to and importance of specific places within the school depending again on the particular context and purpose of the school, and to protect that place with specific behaviors so that its specialness might be maintained, would seem to be important tasks for schools to undertake.

* * *

If the school is to be a sacred space in our collective perception, it simply requires seeing it that way, that is, seeing it through the lens of the sacred. The process begins with firming up the underlying philosophy of education for the school and deciding what, why, and how learning should proceed. From there, the details of architecture can be settled so that form follows function. All schools have perimeters and walls, doors and thresholds, rooms and inner sancta, aids to learning, and furniture. How these are regarded and how they are treated can express a sense of the sacred: that is how they are put to use to open learners to new vistas of understanding, to give them a grounding for life choices to come, to serve as a microcosm of the society we would like to inhabit, an opportunity to be safe and yet challenged to grow and become. Most important of all, above the mere physical features of the school, how its students, teachers, administrators, and supportive community members demonstrate their regard for the space will contribute to the extent of its potency as a sacred space.

CHAPTER 6

Sacred Time

Time is a human construct but has always been part of human understanding of the world and themselves. Time itself does not exist as a natural object although from the beginning it has been inspired by natural phenomena. The rising and setting sun, the phases of the moon, the seasons of the year with alternating warm and cold temperatures, planting and harvesting, monsoons and dry spells, winds alternating from the north, south, east, or west, and birthing and dying have attuned human beings to the passage of time, even though these happenings have not always had an exactness in measurement we would demand today. Nevertheless, these same incidents enabled whole civilizations to order their daily lives.

Our predominant, present construction of time is much more precise. It can be counted in nanoseconds. We wear time machines on our wrists or carry them within our ever-present electronic devices and frame our lives accordingly in hours, minutes, and sometimes seconds. We have built an understanding of time that left the occasions of the rising and setting sun far behind as well as the flexibility and adaptability of those original timekeepers.

We know from experience, however, that not every moment of time, even today, is lived and felt in the same way, and our experiences of it are sometimes more reminiscent of an earlier age before the clock. It is another of what van Manen identifies as a "lifeworld existential"; that is, "temporality." We live time; it is a "way of being in the world."[146] As the ancient wisdom declares:

> *For everything there is a season, and a time for every matter under heaven: a time to be born, and a time to die; a time to plant, and a time to pluck up what is planted; a time to kill, and a time to heal; a time to break down, and a time*

> *to build up; a time to weep, and a time to laugh; a time to mourn, and a time to dance; a time to cast away stones, and a time to gather stones together; a time to embrace, and a time to refrain from embracing; a time to seek, and a time to lose; a time to keep, and a time to cast away; a time to rend, and a time to sew; a time to keep silence, and a time to speak; a time to love, and a time to hate; a time for war, and a time for peace.*[147]

Most of time is lived subjectively. Sometimes the hours or days or years move inexorably slowly; other times when they have slipped by so fast, we can scarcely believe it. Time has a way of expanding or contracting as circumstances determine, making its passage seem more natural and less contrived. Van der Merwe and Habron found that time in the sacred realm is connected with the sense of journey or continuing progress, "flow" (after Mihaly Csikszentmihalyi), and the joy and fulfillment that follows successfully meeting a challenge.[148]

Schools have their own rhythms that impact the experience of passing time during the school year, school day, or even a class period. Even though these divisions of time move inevitably forward, there are beginnings and endings, high points and low, busy times and slow, changing expectations and accomplishments, and breaks and disruptions.

There are occasions when a break in the rhythm of the school day (or year) comes unexpectedly and other times when it is planned and purposeful. The possibility of different experiences of time holds great moment for teachers who are interested in nurturing meaning-making in the lives of their students. In essence, deep learning depends on awareness and realization: being mindful, reflective, and probing for comprehension. These kinds of experiences are as much or even more often sensed at the time of their occurrence than they can be articulated in words. The teacher's role then becomes one of allowing moments of reflection and response to learning even when they do not fulfill the lesson's objectives for that day, recognizing when these instants are possible, and drawing attention to them in ways that invite students to take them in. Such teaching amounts to moving away from the technical, theoretical, and practical elements for a while and into the existential.[149] It means being immersed in the content under study and a maturing of understanding. These occasions make time sacred.

Consequences and Coincidences of Clock Time

The present predominant construct of time is clock time, by some known as "metronomic time."[150] The ticking of minutes and hours in identical increments is predictable, measurable, and relentless. Our lives and those of our students are organized and controlled by class timetables, assignment deadlines, bus schedules, homework due-by dates, sports practice rosters, music lesson appointments, term calendars, and to-do-lists. These organizers are masters of our days and brook little or no resistance. As June Boyce-Tillman has declared, the bell rings and the class lesson stops, regardless of whether the thought processes engendered by the learning activities have been completed or not.[151] The term ends and the examinations begin regardless of whether all the students with their variety of learning styles and abilities have brought their studies to completion or not.

Of course, clock time makes an essential contribution to a well-ordered school and society, for smooth-running organizations, and to meeting expectations. Our collective productivity and efficiency are enhanced by timetables and deadlines. In fact, clocks may well be one of the most significant means that lifted us out of the agrarian age and into the industrial and technological age. These time-measuring instruments encourage focus and production.

However, whether purely coincidental, or causal, or co-determinant, the mechanistic measurement of time that dominates our lives also characterizes an age that is identified as anti-intellectual. Clock time focuses on product rather than process by insisting on time allocations and deadlines. The processes of creativity, analysis, critical thinking, studying, reviewing, evaluating, speculating, reflecting, and imagining get short shrift when the schedule sets a date certain when the process must be completed and a product generated. Reflective thinkers can produce too, but often their products are not utilitarian, material, or immediately relevant, and to the dismay of timetablers, the time needed for arriving at their kinds of products is so often unpredictable and capricious, or, worse, annoyingly uncontrollable when deadlines are mandated. Paradoxically, our products are also better when creative and critical reflection, unbound by the constraints of time, have been part of the process.

Of course, some of the most creative people, including Maya Angelou, W. H. Auden, Anthony Trollope, and others, kept to very strict, even grueling, time and/or production schedules for their writing, as Mason Currey describes in *Daily Rituals: How Artists Work*.[152] But they were making sure they scheduled in their creative work, protecting it from being scheduled out by the relentlessly ticking clock in the service of merely materialistic ends. And they seldom put deadlines on when a project was to be finished; they were simply protecting the time for the process to work. Unfortunately, a love of learning and practice of the creative skills does not have much room in a world that is rushing hour by measured hour toward yet another deadline.

In schools, perpetual motion toward production is manifested in strictly regulating learning outcomes and assessment-driven approaches to teaching and learning so that the product of education meets the goal of generating employable citizens to fill the positions the time-driven economy needs. Too often, wealth has become the ultimate and unquestioned goal toward which all measured minutes and hours are being driven. The 9–5 workday, five days a week, determined by hard-won labor acts of the past has become the new 24/7 on-task requirement with the expectation that work demands can come and go even during the evening and throughout the night, weekends, and vacation times of many workers today. The ticking clock of capitalism never rests. There is little time left for serendipitous learning and non-utilitarian knowledge.

Despite what else we might know and feel about organized religion, with its loss we are also fast losing one of the places that could give us an alternative to secular, mechanized time: the experience of sacred time, that has its own qualities and meanings and that can counteract some of the influence of clock time and expand our spheres of thought and action. While there is evidence of spiritual practices which are more personal and tend to draw on and combine a variety of sources,[153] the traditional religions of the Western world are decreasingly likely to serve their conventional role of spiritual nurture for the majority of the population. This is particularly ironic since it was Benedictine monks who invented the first mechanical clock to help them keep their appointed hours especially during the night.[154] In effect, they had surrendered to clock time just as the industrial world was also embracing the same kind of a mechanical measurement of minutes.

Precise time keeping and many time-management strategies homogenize all time, its measured increments move us inexorably forward while overriding the moments needed for creative thinking, reflection on values, and spiritual nurture. The schools are complicit in these trends, but maybe not inevitably so, and they may be able to recapture as occasion affords alternatives to secular time in their scheduling, and certainly in their oversight of significant learning moments.

This loss of a break in the relentless rhythm of time passing prompts us to create alternative ways toward making some moments sacred. In other words, purposeful or coincidental disruptions (Eliade named these occasions as "irruptions") in time might not only give us relief, but also opportunities to reflect, create, re-evaluate, and find our center. The efficient operation of our lives and institutions depends on punctuality, reliability, and predictability, but there are, nevertheless, occasions when we can and should allow time itself to melt away and become less insistent. When the regular beat of passing moments is turned off, so to speak, we can create fissures or lulls when the sacred can appear and the materialistic and secular can fade. There are several ways schools, learners, and their teachers can do this.

Wasting Time

We can make time, give time, take time, use time, and find time but we usually regret having to waste time. Time is money. Time is precious. Time is limited. This all makes sense when we understand and speak about time as if it were a commodity. This way of thinking is an inherent aspect of mechanical time. But in this process, the sense of the sacred can be crowded out of our lives—and our schools—because the sacred is not always bound to times certain. The sacred is, as Eliade put it, likely to come as an "irruption," breaking into regular time suddenly, even forcefully.[155]

Anna Della Subin, in an opinion piece entitled "How to Stop Time: A Meditation on Procrastination" with the strapline "It's actually O.K. to resist the gods of productivity," proposes that we replace the myth of Expeditus with that of Oblomov.[156] Expeditus, whose name gave rise to "expedite" and its derivatives, was believed by some to have been an early Christian martyr. As one legend goes, his body had been shipped to some nuns in Paris with the word *expedité* or *spedito* on the packing case, which was intended to indicate that it was to be shipped with all dispatch, but which was taken to be the name of the person whose remains were contained within the package. Expeditus became the patron saint of "emergencies, expeditious solutions, against procrastination, merchants, navigators, programmers, and hackers revolutionaries."[157] Subin notes that Expeditus rose to new attention at the time of the Industrial Revolution "as the tempo of the world accelerated with breathtaking speed."[158]

Oblomov, on the other hand, the main character in Russian novelist Ivan Goncharov's novel of the same name published in 1859, is the epitome of procrastination. Understood as a depiction of the decline of Russian aristocracy, Oblomov is a layabout making little or no contribution to the public good but making an art form of doing nothing. He resigns from his work as a civil servant, lounges about all day between his bed and a sofa, assumes no responsibilities, meets few appointments and then only within his rooms, and gradually falls into poverty and lovelessness, frustratingly unredeemed throughout the entire play.

If the frameworks of sacred and secular times are constructed from myths, Expeditus and Oblomov could serve as the modern equivalents of the ancient gods. Our daily lives are lived under the spell of Expeditus—success is judged in terms of moving forward toward our goals of production as efficiently as possible, taking few if any detours on the way to that destination. That is why Subin summons the figure of Oblomov, even though he represents the "archdemon many of us wrestle with daily." She raises the question: "Why not view procrastination not as a defect, an illness or a sin, but as an act of resistance against the strictures of time and productivity?" "Rather than charge through the day, storming the gates of tomorrow," she asserts a different model that pictures one as reposing "on a perch from which to observe, reflect and question whether the world really needs all those things we feel we ought to get done—like a few more pyramids at Giza."

Just as our agrarian ancestors knew there were times for sowing and times for reaping, so too today's teachers can recognize there are times for their learners to search and discover and times to reflect and assimilate what is found; times for effort to learn and times to rest and be thoughtful about what is learned; times to collect facts and information and times to make meaning out of them; times for acting like Expeditus and times for being more like Oblomov.

Although Oblomov is a stark contrast to Expeditus; however, he also falls short as a figure of sacred time, because he represents an empty, amoral, and sterile time. Sacred time is not vacuous but has qualities that are positive and fruitful. One is not disengaged during a "timeless" moment, but actively alive, thinking, wondering, creating. These intervals can be replete with mindfulness and awareness, at once both an antidote to stress and a pause for recognizing and recentering on what is most important and meaningful.

Procrastination may serve as a necessary entry point to sacred time, because, as Israel Scheffler proposes, by postponing less relevant tasks in favor of more urgent ones, or deferring for now the whole task that lies before one to focus on its immediate first steps can provide relief from and remedy for the overwhelming pressure of completion deadlines.[159] Similarly, he argues that idleness also is not always a so-called "educational sin." Recounting the description of the pupil Albert Einstein's "aversion to the constant drill" of schooling in favor of engaging in "daydreaming and meditative musing," Scheffler also sees potential and effectiveness in changes in pace and demand.[160]

Estelle Jorgensen goes further than Scheffler when she proposes redeeming even sloth from among the educational sins. In unpacking the concept of sloth, she elaborates on several elements that can be viewed in more positive light. One of these elements, procrastination, for one, can allow the free flow of imagination, picturing goals not yet fully envisaged and the possibility of coming upon solutions to problems when all the parts fall into place. Laziness is another, but that too can be a form of restfulness in times of stress and guarantee a place in a busy life for recreation and leisure. Oblomov may have been a figure of the utterly uselessness of a life lived without effort, but periods of uselessness may also be an antidote to demands for constantly fulfilling outcomes and producing measurable outputs. Present-centeredness is another element of sloth Jorgensen identifies. It amounts to a failure to plan and prepare for the future. But when the focus can be turned from time to time onto the now, it may in fact enable "serendipity, idiosyncrasy, surprise, and unpredictability," even joy, enhancing "the quality and richness of present experience." A final element identified in her analysis is parsimony, that is, actions taken that reduce the range of possibilities by focusing on a few.[161] Trying to accomplish less can be a move from productivity to quality, from going big to opening the door to greater intimacy, from making a splash to conserving resources, both human and material.

Slowness is also often seen to be a waste of time. We are urged into busyness and as a result we see students stretched beyond reason to accomplish all that is on their schedule: apart from school hours there is football practice, piano lessons, drama club rehearsals, broadcasting a podcast, and running a small start-up business, while maintaining a GPA as close to 4.0 as possible, while their parents are run ragged ferrying them from place to place to meet appointments. So many of these activities are chosen because they appeal and choices among them have been difficult to make; sometimes the activity is to build a CV to persuade college admission committees. An 18-year-old needing a CV? We also see teachers weary with grading, preparing courses, addressing the needs of individual learners, and sometimes making do in crowded and under-resourced classrooms, and administrators frazzled with public duties, budgets, government mandates, and internal issues and responsibilities.

Maggie Berg and Barbara Seeber write specifically to professors in higher education, who are pressured by teaching loads, analyzing and scoring papers, mentoring students, service activities in the university and local community, the constant need to publish or perish, and the effort involved in tenure and promotion processes. They preface their book, *The Slow Professor*, with two quotes that capture the spirit of our times:

the first from Robert Boice: "Western civilization teaches us that displays of busyness are useful and impressive"; the second from Hillary Rettig, that if we are not rushing from moment to moment, "we're simply not the people we're capable of being."[162]

In contradistinction to these claims, Berg and Seeber declare their own manifesto: "We believe that adopting the principles of "Slow" in our professional practice is an effective way to alleviate work stress, preserve humanistic education, and resist the corporate university."[163] They go on to declare that "[w]e need time to think and so do our students. Time for reflection and open-ended inquiry is not a luxury but is crucial to what we do."[164] They argue that living outside of time, a timeless sense of time, when one can become totally absorbed in a moment of discovery and exploration makes room in the life for creativity, original thinking, and even joy.[165] In other words, it makes room for the sacred. What we may otherwise regard as wasting time may serve as a powerful aid to opening the mind to wonder and awe.

Some teachers deliberately plan free time in the schedule, whether just a few minutes or longer, depending on the age and experience of the class members. It is not meant for playing, talking, or completing a task but for apparently doing nothing. Some students will simply sit and stare into space, some may doodle, others will be running ideas through their minds that might eventuate in a poem or mathematical solution. On a larger scale, time needs to be scheduled into the lives of teachers and students that is not school related. Time in the evenings and weekends should be planned as a change of pace and activity. Vacation times and sabbaticals should be embraced by teachers to open themselves to creativity and reflection.

Other World Times

Another tool education has at hand to disrupt time for a while and admit sacred moments of meaning-making is to take learners into a different time zone. Many studies and extracurricular activities effectively do just that: they can put one temporarily into another period or another rhythm that can open the imagination to surprise and new and significant insights.

Study and participation in the arts in all its forms can be particularly powerful keys to sacred time for they take one out of the here and now. They require imagination, novelty, and speculation and hold the symbols and stories of alternative ways of being and living in the world. When Paul Tillich served as a chaplain on the Western Front, his daily experience was of "mud, blood and death." To escape the reality of that time, he could be found huddled in the dugout, gazing at art magazines by candlelight. Botticelli's *Madonna (and Child) with Singing Angels* was a particular favorite. Although these were only reproductions of great masterpieces, when he was able to see the original Botticelli, he was shaken. "That moment," he recalled, "has ... given me the keys for the interpretation of human existence, brought vital joy and spiritual truth."[166] Some learners may also be sensitive to the impact of a painting, sculpture, or architectural space; others may be invited into such an experience, especially if the art teacher is also attuned to perturbances in time that artworks can generate.

In its unique way, music also exhibits changes in how time is experienced. Merely participating in a music event can be a change in pace from the rest of our lives, a break from utilitarian and time-bound routine. And literally, within a musical work, there can be tempo changes. We not only hear them, but we can feel them as though they are echoed in heartbeat and breath rate. From quick time to slow time, from steady to irregular, we can actually experience these changes in pace auditorily, cognitively, and physically.

Music also operates in a metaphorical domain. The literal elements of irruptions, changes in tempi, and circularity and periodicity can prefigure and point to these same elements in larger life. Susanne Langer has made the argument that the very form of music, its structures and shapes, its developments and turns, express the "form of feeling," the experience of our interior lives. The form of the music allows us to acknowledge, explore, and expand our life of feeling.[167] In other words, the literal elements of music can create metaphorically the passage and shape of sacred time.

Reading can also break into the here and now and take participants into a different time zone and a whole new world of experience from which to reflect on life in its many modes. Readers have been able to walk the dusty streets of ancient Rome, harvest the fields of the lord of the manor with the other peasants, ride into battle with the Crusaders, sail the seas with the Vikings, struggle against the negative forces of contemporary ghetto neighborhoods, or join the crew of a starship to explore new worlds. They can feel the slave owner's lash, the thrill of the first sighting of unknown lands, the hope that comes when a search is successful or a mystery solved, or the endurance through suffering that forms the life of a civil rights activist. When engaging in this other time with its characters and events, one's own priorities begin to fall into place and one's world grows much larger and more inclusive.

Studies in science delve into the secrets of life, energy, infinity and burst out of the narrow confines of the minutes given to the lesson. The very concept of a light year applied to calculating the size of the universe or how far to the nearest star uses time as a measure of distance—a mind teasing concept to say the least. Time is an indispensable part of knowing our natural and physical world and is so often employed in ways that challenge the ticking clock of our daily lives: the time for species to evolve or planets to form, the atom to split, the elephant's gestation period compared with the time for robin hatchlings to fly from the family nest, the acceleration of glacier melt and rising seas. Whether measurements are made in eons or nanoseconds, they come fraught with value and demand a personal and sometimes moral response as one ascertains one's place in the world.

These are just examples of the kinds of "irruptions" into the regular pace of our lives that exposure to learning in any field can bring about, but they can be overlooked. Learning something new is rarely mundane or routine. It can be challenging, stretching muscle and mind, but so absorbing that the learner loses touch with the ticking clock. Csikszentmihalyi identifies such experiences as "flow"; that is, those occasions when one is thoroughly absorbed in a project that one loses the sense of the passage of time. They open one to greater creativity and enjoyment. They are a path not only to happiness but to full consciousness and a measure of control over the inner life.[168] Under these conditions, time becomes less relevant.

Trajectories of Time

In the last chapter of *The Myth of the Eternal Return*, the book he considered his most significant,[169] Eliade most forthrightly addresses the nature of different pathways that time takes in our experience, although even here he feels the subject exceeds the limits of a single chapter.[170] Basically, he describes how time proceeds along two trajectories. One is linear—event succeeding event, relentlessly forward moving, and unstoppable—presumably measured quantitatively; the other circular—repeating, returning, renewing—and sensed qualitatively.

When we move through our days and years in a linear fashion, we create our biography. We may have a narrative that unfolds as time goes by, but essentially time marches on persistently as a backdrop to our decisions and circumstances. On a larger scale, humanity also moves forward in a more-or-less straight line creating history. One thing follows another, one event gives way to another, generations of actors appear on the world stage but surrender that stage to the next generation, usually regardless of overall purpose or plan.

This is the very condition Eliade sees as "the terror of history." Events happen in historical time as mere history, too often terrorizing human beings because what happens seems largely arbitrary and unpredictable.[171] While we may plan for tomorrow, we are not in command of the future. We are trapped in circumstances beyond our full control, and these will roll out eventually with or without our agreement. Present time is subject to the vagaries of times past and times to come. There is no end except obliteration: from birth to death; from the big bang to a black hole. In linear time, we set deadlines and try to meet them; we plan for our future and do our best to prepare for it; and we make predictions about what is to come based on past experience, but through it all, we are trapped in the flow of events that move us forward inexorably and largely uncontrollably.

In contrast, however, a different understanding of time, accepted by the ancients, regards time as circular or repeating, bringing an element of predictability and validation to historic events because it gives a sense that we have been this way before. Time doubles back, returns, and repeats itself. Spring may give way to summer and then to fall and then winter, but it returns in due course. Day may become night, but night becomes day. Linear time, on the other hand, lacks differentiation. Every minute and hour is identical to every other minute and hour if we judge them by the ticking clock, but circular time moves through a cycle of qualitative changes.

According to Eliade, archaic peoples, who lived almost exclusively within this cyclical conception of time, were able to periodically abolish the terror through ritualistic repetition and regeneration. They viewed events against a grand narrative with a coherent metahistorical meaning, "a transcendent model."[172] Because they saw that "historical events depended upon cycles and astral situations, ... [the events] became intelligible and even foreseeable"–they could do so because they reflected and provided "transhistorical justification" for them that was not after all arbitrary.[173]

Since Eliade put such stock on periodicity as a feature of sacred time, it is difficult to dismiss it as irrelevant in our day. In fact, he gives some hints about how contemporary peoples can also enter such a time even though we have moved beyond traditional dependence on the rising and setting sun, the phases of the moon, and the cycle of the seasons.[174] Access to this other kind of time may still be available in the present age, he suggests, through myth and imagination, through art and story and ritual.[175]

A feature of cyclical or sacred time that is prominent in Eliade's analysis of mythic thought is its return to beginnings, *ab initio*, the moment of creation. "Periodic ceremonies," he explains, have been a constant feature of human communities. They serve dual purposes: an "annual expulsion of demons, diseases, and sins" and the ushering in of a new epoch or new phase in the cycle of the year.[176] In archaic cultures, he explains, "the world is renewed annually; in other words, with the start of each year the world can recover its original sanctity."[177] He traces this fundamental idea across times and cultures, concluding that "from one gnosis or one wisdom to another, the immemorial theme of the second birth is enriched with new values, which sometimes profoundly changes the content of the experience,"[178] but it inevitably recurs. Linear time falls out of step with this development and consequently cannot capture its hopefulness.[179]

We live most of our lives in linear time, subconsciously. In the context of school, however, there are also many opportunities to start anew and experience a return to beginnings. Standing out above all is the beginning of a new school year, especially if that beginning takes place as the student moves from one grade level to the next, or from one institution to the next in line. Grade school comes full circle, ends, and high school starts afresh, with renewed focus and challenge. It too ends and college begins, and college becomes graduate school. A similar sense of starting over with new hope and resolution might also accompany the new school term and, with guidance from the school, even a new week or day. Rituals, as we shall see in the next chapter, have an important role in marking these moments of changeover. Beginning a new work project or opening a new book can also feel like a regeneration. This dimension of time allows one to experience the re-invigoration and empowerment that comes from beginning anew.

Eliade did not acknowledge that the "terror of history" can also be a potential element of circular time. Human beings do not have to be like Sisyphus, the legendary character from the Iliad who tried to cheat inevitable death and for his trickery spent eternity hefting a rock up a hill, only to see it roll back down, over and over. We are not doomed to repeating cycles of predictability. If we did end the last cycle with a sense of little accomplishment or low grades or feelings of guilt over our poor effort, it does not mean the new cycle must also end the same way. The escape from this terror may lie in construing the passage of time as a combination of linear and circular that suggests a spiral pathway. Contemporary awareness informs us that we cannot return to *ab initio* because each time we return to the origin having traveled around the circle, we have been changed by our experiences along the way. The starting point for the next venture, a new school year, the next level of school, a new course of study, a new musical work to master is not identical to the last time we were there. It reflects both the forward progress of the past and the beginning of another round of learning. Such an understanding carries hope rather than terror.

To capitalize on the hope and developing self-awareness of these moments of transition, teachers might reflect with their learners on what they had learned of significance about the world, their priorities, and their imagined futures over the recent cycle of learning and how it positions them for the next. Recognizing and celebrating the movement through time and seeing the development of the student not only in terms of a straight line forward but also as a series of fresh starts can add attention and potency to the learning that will take place. Self-understanding, renewable hope, and resilience in the face of the terror of history with its past disappointments, failures, and alienations, could flourish.

* * *

Time is sacred when moments are transformative, when the heart considers larger meanings, or the mind absorbs new and grander truths. Capturing some sacred time in the school schedule and curriculum that is presently dominated by the mechanistic measuring beat of the clock does not seem all that difficult. When teachers and educational leadership plan for alternative rhythms to the incessant striving to meet learning objectives, celebrate moments of new beginnings, and open up to the unexpected and serendipitous through the arts, music, and other studies, different ways of understanding and being in the world can gain admission and unlock the possibility of fresh arenas for thought and action. If we can live on occasion in sacred time and invite our students to join us there, the impact could be momentous. Materialistic ends would assume a lower value, the full range of the life of mind and heart a higher value. The schools could become enveloped in grander purposes and purveyors of genuine learning.

CHAPTER 7

Rituals, Memorials, and Sacred Objects

On the first Monday I was in Grade 3, all the pupils in my grade and higher at the Tyler Street State School in suburban Melbourne, Australia were gathered around the flagpole in the school's quadrangle. Collected there with "thousands" of others (in reality, maybe a couple of hundred), we watched as *my* teacher, Mr. McLean, limped across with a straight-back chair under his arm. His limp, it was rumored, was the result of a war wound. He climbed up onto the chair, drew a large, white handkerchief from his coat pocket, and conducted us as we sang the national anthem, which was at that time, "God save the Queen." This was my induction into the "big people's" grades, for those in "bubs," what we commonly called K-2, did not participate in this ritual.

Within that flag-raising ceremony are all the aspects of ritual as a sacred endeavor. It was awesome: I was a little individual in a mass of children and singing voices. It was somewhat terrifying (*tremendum*) but appealing (*fascinans*) at the same time. It was conducted at a special time and in a special place; at least, it made that particular space just for that particular moment in time special and different from what went before and what would come after as the quadrangle again became our playground. It was a period of transition from "bubs" to "big people;" an initiation or a rite of passage so to speak into a new understanding of ourselves and our place in our little universe. It connected us with our classmates and peers, and all the other school children and young people in other quadrangles across the country who were doing the same thing at the same time. It clarified and reinforced the values of patriotism and sacrifice in the service of freedom and security. Mr. McLean's war wound was a memorial to the war that had been won and evil routed but not without pain and loss. Did I understand all that on the first Monday in Grade 3? Of course not, but that moment and the recurring flag-raising ceremonies began a process of meaning-making that I have been able to elaborate and critically reflect on over the succeeding decades.

The Monday morning ritual also centered on the flagpole, a sacred memorial, and the flag, a sacred object, with its Union Jack in the left top-most corner representing Australia's historic ties with Britain. The Union Jack, with its overlying crosses of St. George (for England), St. Patrick (for Ireland), and St. Andrew (for Scotland) speaks not merely of England but of the United Kingdom as it was at that time and our connection with it. The flag also includes a representation of the Southern Cross constellation seen clearly in skies south of the equator, so it was uniquely representative of our geographical location on the globe, and the large seven-pointed star for the six states and the Northern Territory that comprise the country. We were well acquainted with the flag and its various parts having been through the drawing classes that had us reproduce it in crayon, which was not easy especially when you look closely and see that the red and white stripes on the Union Jack are not all the same width! Altogether, the flag was a venerated object that grounded us in the larger world we occupied.

Part of the potency of rituals lies in the possibility that as symbolic performances, they can be multivocal and are almost always suggestively metaphorical. From Israel Scheffler's work, we can propose that they can *denote*; that is, point out something to be noticed and remembered, just as our flag-raising ritual and the flag itself denoted country, patriotism, sacrifice, victory. They can *exemplify*; that is, serve as a sample of something much larger, such as respect and loyalty to the queen and country in this case. Mr. McLean and his war wound and his lead in conducting the singing were an exemplification of those values. Rituals can *express*; that is, provide an opportunity for acting out one's feelings and commitments, as we certainly did by lustily singing the national anthem. They can *re-enact*, that is, metaphorically reproduce a significant moment; in our case, Governor Philip and the original white settlers planting the first British flag on Australian soil and the installation of the first Australian flag at Federation, both moments to be recalled by following generations of both original peoples and successive waves of immigrants—a history to be remembered with both joy and regret. Each re-enactment connects the performer with similar performances of the past and present. Re-enactment, then, builds traditions and community at the same time—as long as it symbolizes the sentiments of an increasingly diverse community.[180]

Throughout his writings, Mircea Eliade proposed that rituals re-enacted the founding of the cosmos for traditional peoples, so engaging in a ritual signified a re-forming of the world as these peoples understood it.[181] What lingers today is the sense that a ritual can still mark a re-creation and a new beginning: renewing who one might be and how that understanding can be lived out going forward. The many symbolizing features of rituals make them a powerful force in a community. On another dimension, Harvey Cox describes ritual as a source of fantasy by providing a formal structure for make-believe, opening access to a wealth of human feeling and nourishing and embodying society's imagination.[182] Such claims give ritual an important place not only when one thinks of society at large but also of the school setting.

Keeping alive the imaginative and creative elements of ritual making and performing becomes an important challenge for teachers and administrators in several immediate ways. One challenge may involve finding a balance between preparing students for a ritual and yet allowing for surprise elements when the ritual occurs. In my case, although I was well prepared to respect the flag, I have no recollection of being told what the Monday morning flag-raising ritual was about and what was expected of me, so I felt unimpeded to experience the full impact of its *fascinans et tremendum*.

Another challenge lies in allowing sufficient flexibility and adaptability for reviewing and reforming old rituals and perhaps creating new ones. Rituals are conserving—they stabilize and preserve collective understandings. This may well be their greatest strength, but also their greatest weakness in that they can foreclose new understandings and fresh viewpoints. The Australian national flag, for instance, failed to represent the lives and experiences of the country's original people and, in fact, was a reminder of the impact of imperialism on their way of life and identity. Their efforts led to the creation of a new indigenous flag in 1971 to be flown together with the national one. This new flag reflects the connection between the people and the land as well as their distinction from the first English colonizers.[183] To remain effective, therefore, a ritual needs to be reviewed and reevaluated and possibly reclaimed in new dress to remain cogent as the context or the community changes.

To understand ritual from a sociological perspective, Randall Collins builds on the initial work of Émile Durkheim and others to propose a theory of "interaction ritual chains," that is, the sequence of social situations where circumstances, formal and informal, make us who we are.[184] Rather than focus on an individual's agency in making a life, the theory draws attention to a person's social interactions that link in chains with various branches and cross-overs contributing to her uniqueness and development. In ritual, Collins sees the power of bringing people together, engaging them emotionally, and providing the group with meaningful symbols. For this to happen, a ritual must possess four essential ingredients: group assembly, a barrier to outsiders, mutual focus of attention, and a shared mood. Then it can give rise to four outcomes: group solidarity, emotional energy, symbols or sacred objects, and standards of morality.[185]

We can see all the features Collins identifies in a simple school ritual. One teacher was able to transform the requirement of lining up before entering the classroom, a familiar routine we see in schools every day, into something more than an aimless practice. She drew up a legend and posted it at eyelevel for her students at the doorway to the classroom. It listed the ways a teacher may appropriately greet her charges: a hug, a pat on the shoulder, a smile, a handshake, a nod, or no response at all. As each child passed by, he could choose how the teacher would greet him by tapping on one of the alternatives. This simple device gave class members a sense of personal power and demanded of them some thought and choice in what could otherwise be simply a predictable routine. As Collins notes, the ritual encompassed a bodily presence and gathering of participants in a socially interactive situation, the teacher and her charges. Those who were not entering the classroom were excluded from the ritual—hugs, pats, and handshakes were reserved for the students. Everyone paid attention—there was no entry without passing through the portal and choosing a greeting style. And although the activity permitted the students to reveal what they felt they would like from the teacher on any particular day, the real effect of the ritual was that all participants shared an emotional and apparently joyous space at that moment.

The "outcomes" of sharing in the ritual included a heightened emotional state and energy (a positive way to start the school day for these young learners), a sense of belonging and inclusion in the group, a mutual sacred symbol (the list of possible greetings and the greetings themselves), and a commitment, even a moral obligation, to the ritual itself and the class (outrage may well have followed if the ritual had been banned or made fun of.)[186] A ritual, then, is a lived activity in a social situation, engaging body, mind, and heart.

When one is not present physically and a ritual situation comes via the media, for instance, something of the impact is reduced.[187] Teachers who were forced to conduct class online during the 2019–2022 COVID-19 pandemic found this to be true and had to seek alternatives to maintain group cohesion and emotional engagement. Online classes may need to envisage new rituals that place the body virtually in contact with the group. Collins also acknowledges that rituals can be unsuccessful: they can fail when they do not create "emotional effervescence," or when they have become empty of meaning, boring, and interaction fatigue has set in, or they no longer contribute to group solidarity, or when they are forced on unwilling participants.[188]

It is not difficult to imagine that some individuals are simply going through the motions without any of the salutary effects others may be experiencing in the same situation. In fact, some may actively resist being fully engaged in an activity for any one of a number of reasons, from set personal priorities or refusal to accept the premises of the ritual to being simply ornery or cantankerous. A child in the lineup for entering the classroom may have had an upsetting start to the day at home or a fight with classmates that left him feeling alienated from class activities. So, for an individual, an activity may be experienced as a ritual with deep meaning while for another it is something one does because it is inescapable or customary. While Collins' focus is on situations rather than individuals, he recognizes the uniqueness of the individual, seeing it as the product of an individual having gone through her own interaction ritual chains.[189]

We might use the theory to propose a line of demarcation between a ritual and a mere habit or a custom. When a repeated action continues to spark the imagination, carries meaning and motivation within it, and demands a level of mindfulness, then it may serve as a ritual for an individual within a group. Without these elements, the activity is a failed ritual.

From a social interactionist perspective, a repeated activity outside of a group experience does not rise to the level of ritual because it lacks the shared emotion and sacred symbolism that comes with group interaction. Such a repetition can, however, be strong in personal feeling and energy, passionately protected, and rooted in a sense of one's place in the world. It may be lacking in social interaction, but it does involve bodily engagement and according to Collins it may come about as a result of previous chains of encounters and frames future social situations. Some teachers, for example, develop private rituals to prepare themselves for teaching. Shona Simkin reports in the *Harvard Gazette* the personal rituals some teachers in the Business School have developed for themselves: one always carries a leather binder he has taken to class for 25 years; another makes copious notes on things she should take into the classroom, words she needs practice pronouncing, her outline for the chalkboard, who she is planning to call on during the class, and so on. In this instance, she does not look at the notes once the lesson begins but is comforted by the fact that they are there. Another prepares a spreadsheet of the students in the class and various facts about each one of the learners, so he knows the class members at least a little before he teaches them. Yet another "hermits" herself before class to ready herself and her approach, predicting among other things possible tension points so that her response material is "loaded into working memory."[190] As his teaching assistant, I was walking with my professor to the first lecture of the new school year when he confessed to a calming mantra he recites to himself: "This is not my first lecture; this is my [three hundred and fifty-third] lecture." Teachers in other educational situations no doubt have their personal rituals before class begins. These are not easily dismissed because they are conducted in private, because they do have social implications.

The documentary movie, *Pianoforte*,[191] portrays the participants offstage in the Chopin Piano Competition and the private rituals they undertake to prepare body and mind before their performance in front of the audience and judges. Among the activities we see pacing, exercising, socializing, retreating, laughing, crying, listening to recordings or teachers, practicing, eating, and not eating—a range of repeated and yet individualized behaviors to calm anxiety and ready body and mind for the performance. The same kind of ritualized behaviors characterize many learners preparing for final exams or a football match or presenting a project to the class for review. In each case, there is action, focused emotion, barriers to protect privacy, symbols such as mantras, mental images, and sacred objects all of which create an emotional effervescence and motivation when the individual returns to the group. Such individualized rituals can provide predictability and bring a measure of calm, control, and groundedness before fronting up for a challenge. They may strike one as being simply idiosyncratic or even superstitious behavior, and unfortunately, some may even become pathological, but they should not be so readily dismissed. Their efficacy may rest on the fact that they can bolster confidence which in turn can lead to success.[192]

Rituals may be present but not recognized as such, especially when teachers and their supporters are consumed with organizing an event with ritual potential. The preparation that goes into some rituals can be challenging but also onerous, consuming an inordinate amount of resources, human and material. Participants can be dazzled with the spectacle but lose a sense of the moment. Some reflection on the purposes of a particular ritual, whether it be small and serve a lesser purpose or weighted with deeper unrecognized significance, may reveal how best to plan for and structure the event to maximize its meaning-making potential.

In the same way, memorials and sacred objects are likely to be all around a school community, but they may not be recognized as such or accessed for their sacred contribution. One thinks of honor rolls, citations, trophies, photographs, festivals, competitions, award showcases, banners, flags, codes of conduct, mottoes, and school songs, for instance. Galleries featuring student artworks and performances by the school orchestra, band, or choir and student theater productions may memorialize student achievement and talent, not to mention their concentrated effort and hours of practice. The same may be said of the sports and debating teams. Martin Luther King Jr. Day, the third Monday in January, is memorialized actively in the United States as a day for community service and many schools organize the day for that purpose. Sometimes the very naming of a school is a memorial to a significant person or event and makes the school bearing that name a sacred object in itself. I drive past a school that proudly displays its name as the Marguerite E. Small Elementary School and I wonder who Ms. Small was and what she is remembered for, and whether the students and teachers in that school know the answers to those musings and celebrate them.[193]

In line with sacred traditions, schools too have their secrets and mysteries. I remember being in Grade 4 in my new one-teacher school and hearing Grade 5 tackling the inscrutabilities of long division. I could not wait for the day when we too would be inducted into that mystery with its strange maneuvers and rows of numbers. One wonders what difference it would make if the syllabus were to be seen as more than a chronological series of learning outcomes to be fulfilled, assignments to be undertaken and evaluated, and topics to be mastered. If it were also seen as a series of mysteries to be explored and secrets to be penetrated, what effect might that have on motivation and inspiration? Maybe then, we would not have to respond so often to the frequently heard complaint: Why do we have to learn this stuff?

Unpacking the roles of ritual and its associated venerated objects, memorials, and secrets indicates that they make several specific contributions that in many cases they alone can make. In the course of a school day, or semester, or year, many community-wide rituals will mark the times and places as sacred for learners, teachers, and their supporting publics.

Rituals for Community Building

In describing interaction ritual chains, Collins places the group at the center of his theory: the group comes together physically, shares emotional responses and energy, and coheres to include everyone. In effect, he is elaborating on the foundational work of earlier social interaction theorists. In his investigation of original societies, Durkheim, for instance, saw the potency of ritual as a community builder. He concluded that social life needs its rituals if it wants to even continue to exist. The first effect of ritual, he observed, was in bringing people together, thus making them "more intimate with one another," and "multiply[ing] the relations among them." In other words, rituals provide a significant thread connecting members of the community as they act and feel something in common. The net result of this connective thread, Durkheim concluded, was to give participants a feeling of belonging and hence of well-being. He pressed further by claiming that rituals also help to "reforge their moral nature" at the same time for, in important ways, ritual brings attention to foundational beliefs and shared values.[194]

In that vein, Robert Trumpbour notes the connection of present rituals with past events. Drawing on what went before helps endow the present with meaning, he suggests, even though this may involve a selective memory of the past. Myth and storytelling are implicated then as a basis for participation in ritual.[195] It is possible that literalizing and laying open for critique, the historical and sometimes fanciful accounts of the origins of a ritual, might undermine the assumed facts that lie at its foundation but that might not matter anyway. At my alma mater is a small monument announcing that some yards east, the founders had found a sign in the ground, a small, plowed row in otherwise untilled land, that led to choosing this particular site for the college. The row had great significance since it had appeared in a dream beforehand. Recent scholarship suggests that such a sign had not actually appeared. Despite such revelations, the story is still accepted as true at some level but only in the sense that the founding of the college in this place at that time was providential. Paradoxically, when the realities of the past are taken non-literally or metaphorically, factual revelations to the contrary may not necessarily destroy the potency of the ritual or memorial itself.

Religious services provided common ground at one time for large numbers of community members and still does for many, but as the churches continue to lose members, other more secular rituals have come to fill that need. Musical performances, sports events, movies, and other media,[196] clubs, and so on are imbued with ritual elements. In a classical music concert, for instance, the members of the orchestra wear prescribed clothing (as seriously considered although not usually as ornate as the robes for religious officiates) and the audience dresses in particular ways deemed appropriate for the occasion. There are routines and times for entry on and exit off stage, tuning up, and acknowledging audience applause. A popular music concert too has its own rituals again involving dress, how fans respond, the play of lights, and so on. Stadiums across times and cultures have historically been significant sites for rituals around athletic events, musical performances, and patriotic gatherings.[197] Certainly there are well defined rituals that make up part of the experience of attending a football match or a baseball game and can include opening anthems, chants, totemic-like creatures or mascots, and wearing particular clothes and colors. When fans can join a sea of red shirts, blue and yellow stripes, or green caps, they know they belong and become a part of the team.

Within the school, there are identifiable rituals. How instruments are distributed for music lessons, what to wear in workshop or science lab or physical education, how to address the teacher, how to move along the corridors, how to line up for the school bus, and so it goes. When it comes down to it, so much school behavior is ritualized in small predetermined and repeated actions. Routines like this make for easier management of the school environment and all those within it. Young students in particular whose family life is chaotic find a measure of predictability and stability in these kinds of routines, just as positive family rituals have been shown to promote social connectedness and act as a buffer against depression and anxiety.[198]

More significantly, classroom interactions can be arranged with the intention of recognizing and employing students' bodily presence, engaging their emotional commitments, and setting a boundary that is inclusive and protective of all to build cohesion and shared motivational energy within the group. In *Ritualised Belonging,* music educators and their students describe how they have created rituals in making music together and in performing music for others.[199] Such possibilities present themselves wherever learners and teachers can interact in shared space. Teamwork on a science project or mounting a play or visiting a zoo on a class excursion are events imbued with ritualized elements that determine how learners will prepare for, engage in, and follow up on the event itself.

On a larger scale, and perhaps closer to our common understanding of ritual, are the events like the opening and closing of a school year, term, or week, commencement exercises, homecomings, founders' days, prom nights, and days of service. These are usually intended to set a tone to inspire learning and commitment to the values of the school and often mark a milestone in the experience of growing up. They may involve wearing full academic robes, processionals, rousing music, and stirring speeches. Rituals may also be as simple as the one I witnessed as I drove past the local elementary school on the last day of the school year. All the staff had gathered on the front lawn and as each school bus pulled out, they waved goodbye to their students and the students waved back. It was moving to witness, and I can imagine how moving it was for these young learners and for the staff. It marked an endpoint, a closure to a shared experience, but also underscored the sense of unity and the warmth in that school community that would be carried forward in the weeks ahead.

In many schools, sports events also readily fall into the ritual category. The school team identifies heroes, and the uniforms, the playing of the school band, the awards, the athleticism, the animated cheer leaders, the entry and exit of the teams from the field, all combine for many in building school spirit. They can also be sites to enact the values of teamwork and good sportsmanship.

Cox finds ritual to be a liberating force since it can release the imagination—but only if it is not enforced. If participation is required of community members, he suggests, it would "choke off spontaneity" and become nothing more than ideology giving rise to a "spurious unity."[200] As a third-grader, I had no choice about attending the flag-raising ceremony but fortunately for me and my peers, requiring attendance in this particular ritual at this particular time in history presented no noticeable problems, but today, participation in that ritual is less frequently mandated. Peer or teacher pressure may negate the imaginative liberation and community building of ritual engagement when compelling non-conforming students to participate.

Durkheim has been criticized for seeing society and its rituals in monolithic terms that do not accommodate so well the size or variety of a contemporary populace. Not everybody in a community attends the same religious services, follows the same sports team, or goes to the same concerts even though many do. And not everyone in a school setting engages with the same enthusiasm in sports events, academic processionals, or school music performances. Some students will intentionally avoid some school events for religious reasons or personal preferences. And yet, subgroups within a society or school may have their own rituals which can be equally effective in building community within their smaller enclave.[201] In a large university, with a substantial College of Arts and Sciences, boasting a strong literature program, a group of learners who tried their hand at writing poetry lived in the same residence hall on campus. They were a very small group within a very large university community, yet they created an annual ritual for themselves, "Naked Poetry Reading." As the name suggests, the attendees arrived wrapped in nothing more than bed sheets which were discarded when all had assembled. Reading their compositions to others while undressed represented for them the baring of one's soul to others when one writes poetry, a celebration of authenticity, honesty, openness, and the vulnerability that comes with writing. The ritual was a powerful bodily metaphor for them, designed by them and conducted with dignity and decorum. In other instances, other subgroups made up of athletes as well as artists, music makers, debaters, computer devotees, and other interest groups in the school can be nurtured in smaller, more intimate groups toward school spirit with their own heroes, enactments, memorials, and celebrations.

Because a single ritual focuses on a specified and limited range of values, many rituals may be necessary, but then this may create the possibility that elements of one ritual will conflict with that of another.[202] An event that celebrates an academic or athletic achievement may need to reconcile the values of individual accomplishment, winning, and good fortune with other events that deal with team effort, losing, disciplined practice, and preparation. Communities and schools come to need more than one ritual to capture a range of values which in itself leaves open the need for reflection and discussion.

Rituals for Healing and Grieving

Anthropologic literature is replete with descriptions of rituals intended to promote healing. While modern medicine has lured contemporary

Western societies away from many of these practices, all healing is not only for physical maladies. Healing of the psyche or soul, where inner agony and pain, grief and anxiety can exist, is also an important path to wellness, especially since body, mind, and soul are inextricably interlaced.

Within a school community, as in the larger community, trauma comes uninvited in the form of death, crippling disease, accident, or other kind of loss. So too does damage and hurt in the homes of many students who bring their aching hearts or resentments and anger to school with them. Violence takes its toll; gun violence in particular has become the most common cause of the death of children in the US.[203] Teen suicide rates are alarming, with numbers increasing in the country year by year with no sign of abating.[204] Serious efforts at healing are urgently needed and, when words fail us, it is possible to see a role for ritual in the process of healing mind and body and opening spaces for communal grieving.

June Boyce-Tillman's study of healing suggests that indigenous practices, Eastern philosophy, and New Age thinking have merged and melded to create processes involving dance, music, focused daydreaming, meditation, and other elements for confronting and addressing physical and mental health issues for individuals and groups. Modern, allopathic medicine, that is medicine that uses opposing drugs in the treatment of disease, applied alone does not always have the same salutary effect as these more wholistic approaches, a gap that alternative, ritualized healing may fill, she explains.[205] These general processes may need to be adapted specifically for the school setting, keeping in mind that what might be appropriate for an individual may not fit so well with the needs of the larger group. Starhawk underscores the importance of involving potential participants in the creation of a ritual especially when borrowing from another tradition so that it does not become "pompous" and "clichéd."[206]

A healing or grieving ritual may serve many purposes: it may honor the embodiment of a value or goal, celebrate a sense of self-worth, confront the cause of distress and symbolically represent its overthrow, or it may simply provide a moment for reflecting with others so one feels less alone in the emotional turmoil of loss. Frequently a traumatized community at school or beyond will hold a candlelight vigil and create a temporary memorial honoring what or who is lost. Sadly, many of us have attended such gatherings where we have permission to weep in public and be moved by the weeping of others. To weep together, to put our arms around another, to shine a light with them on the tragedy in its bleak finality and even senselessness is to find a measure of strength and relief.

Ritual can be a meeting place for doing and feeling that can give rise to meaning-making. When judiciously added to the school program, it can encourage participants to reflect on the larger matters of life and death, heroes, and priorities. It can provide an opportunity for them to reassess their place in the school and the world at large and commit to enduring values. In other words, not only is community strengthened as healing is addressed and communally experienced grief is shared and expressed, but learners can for that short span of time at least transcend[207] the trivialities and anxieties of ordinary life and begin to grasp what is beyond words, the "ultimate," and "really real."[208]

Choosing a ritual can be a fraught process. For example, some prefer to mourn alone; others may be urged to participate before they are ready to face a loss; still others may have a ritual preference they can comfortably share with other mourners. To be effective, the ritual needs to be expressive and employ symbols that capture the emotion and meaning of a loss. Chris van Rhyn reflects on the ritual process he engaged in at the death of his mother. It was not something that came spontaneously but it took several years before it reached the point of expression. His ritual was to compose an electronic work based on Emily Dickinson's "Because I could not Stop for Death." Composing this work was aesthetically pleasing for him and tapped into the archetype of the Mother goddess symbol within his psyche.[209] It was not an action he could hurry or force, and it needed to be his own articulation. Within the social setting of the school, a community of mourners may share a ritual with all the benefits that come from the sharing: a sense of group belonging, a commonly acceptable symbol system and its meaning, collective emotional intensity, and mutual commitment to the ritual and its moral underpinnings. But room needs also to be made for more personal and individual rituals when the time is right for the mourner.

Within this type of ritual lies another that June Boyce-Tillman calls rituals for reconciliation.[210] We have seen ritual elements in the annual

National Sorry Day in Australia when the populace recalls and reflects on the history of how indigenous peoples have been treated, especially in the removal of indigenous children from their homes to be re-educated in approved boarding schools. These occasions remind Australians that acts of violence are not only in the distant past but can be reflected today when children are removed under the auspices of child welfare. On May 26 each year the nation finds ways to remember and apologize. National Days of Truth and Reconciliation have also been commemorated in Canada, and in the United States, the National Native American Day and the celebration of Juneteenth have a similar function. When the ritual leads to action, the community can heal and rebuild. Bringing together students from different ethnic groups, the way Jewish and Palestinian young people have met, studied, worked and played together at summer camps and out-of-country schools, provides settings for rituals of reconciliation. Within the school, antagonism can arise between factions of teenagers and scuffles can break out between children. Teachers can use age-appropriate ceremonies, including everything from simple handshakes to follow-up activities after group discussions that encourage not only blame but admissions of guilt. When the time is right, reconciliation involves acknowledging wrongdoing, compensating for past injustices where possible, and finding better ways of moving forward.

Rituals for Change

A transformation in learners' understanding of themselves and what is of most worth can in turn lead to further reactions which can be ritualized: that is, actions toward change. The students in Parkland, Florida who escaped with their lives in the horrific shooting at their school and the parents of children slain at school in New Haven, Connecticut grieved individually and collectively, but their healing was nurtured forward and transformed into action. They began with organized protests which were picked up and multiplied across the country and beyond to demand change in gun laws and have been followed up with political action on many fronts.

Theologians and ethicists in womanist and Black theology use the phrase, "rituals of resistance,"[211] to identify actions and events intended to bring about change. Hanna Nikkanen and Heidi Westerlund describe how such rituals can express, create, and maintain the values of the school and reveal the hierarchies and power relations in effect in society and within the school that need to be understood and addressed. In the process, the participants can learn to trust themselves and develop their negotiating skills.[212] While gun laws have not been significantly revised, the efforts of the protesters may seem to have been wasted, but the participants themselves are changed by doing something rather than nothing in taking a stand and defending and promoting it. Nikkanen and Westerlund underscore the salutary impact on the participants that is possible in engaging in a ritual for change especially when students and their teachers critically and collegially reflect on what they experience during a ritual performance and its effect not only within the school but beyond.[213] The reflection itself can also serve as a starting point for reviewing, improving, and changing the ritual itself.

Rites of Passage

School life at its various stages is bookended with rites of passage, those markers for significant moments of transition from one recognizable stage to another. A bookend marking the close of one stage often serves as the bookend marking the beginning of the next.

When I and my school mates together moved from "bubs" to Grade 3, attendance at the flag-raising ceremony and the change from sitting at kindergarten tables into real desks marked the transition from one set of expectations and responsibilities to another: we would now need to show more self-discipline and pay closer attention and tackle higher levels of learning which our growing up made possible. Graduation from high school marks the end of adolescence/post-adolescence with its angst about sorting out the self and taking on greater independence. For students in non-academic tracks, rituals for entering apprenticeships or new work and/or study environments can also be considered to mark the passage. Graduation from university marks the end of studies and preparing for a career and entering into the workforce, establishing a family, procuring a mortgage, paying off student loans, and so on. The rituals that attend these transitions are moments of celebration that are full of feeling for both observers and participants, including possibly a level of nostalgia for what has passed and anxiety about what is to come. Fortunately, few learners shrink from these transitions even when all the questions about their future direction have not been answered. Those who do not or cannot move from one stage to the next become the focus of concern, rightly or wrongly, for family and friends and possibly professional counselors.

Rites of passage in traditional societies amplified the aspects of a transition. Frequently the young person had no choice but was taken by force by the elders and submitted to the process. There was often fear, pain, a period of isolation and abandonment, disfigurement, or an endurance test of some kind. Achieving manhood or womanhood, with the rights and privileges it may afford, was not won lightly.

Vestiges of these elements have not disappeared in our kinder, gentler processes but may simply be more muted. Years of study culminating in examinations are endured before graduation. Sometimes agonizing choices about career paths, life partners, where to live, and so on have had to be made. Uncertainty about the future may prevail. Being forced to leave behind the familiar and face the unknown is not always welcome. Growing independence may also bear traces of feelings of abandonment. A graduation, a passing-out parade, or an awards ceremony are all comparable to being removed from one familiar environment with its expectations and set of personal relationships into another. It resembles the eventual return of initiates to the tribe as fully-fledged individuals: it is an opportunity to celebrate their achievement and welcome them into the next level of growing up. There is also something inevitable about passing from one stage to the next; there is no room for choice and the transition must be endured.

Rites of passage come with a measure of emotion. A commencement may be awesome, joyful, and experienced as a transcendence into a new level of self-understanding. It may also come with feelings of self-doubt, sadness, or a reticence to accept what is next. For many, the transition is marked with hope and nostalgia, eager anticipation and a sense of loss. The feelings that come with these occasions are revelatory and can be prompts to greater self-awareness.

On the negative side, hazing rituals show just how deeply rites of passage rely on processes that echo the distant past in contemporary society. They can include humiliating behaviors that reinforce the hierarchy of the group the initiate is about to enter so that their place in the new system is clear. They may involve physical or psychological pain or a test of endurance. They are inescapable if one wants to belong to the group, for they serve as the sole "gateway" to membership. They are also self-perpetuating, for even those previously hazed supervise future hazings despite their own bad memories. Hazing practices are actively discouraged in school settings not only because they can be dangerous or even fatal, but studies have also shown that they can actually negate the sense of community and comradeship they purport to support. Celebratory orientations are more effective gateways than hazings; they move away from being dysfunctional, violent, and traumatizing into being a supportive, mentoring, inclusive way of welcoming a new member into the group.[214] They do not have to be just a recital of things to know and places to be in the new setting but can be designed to give the "initiates" a taste of good things to come, a celebration of community and what it stands for, and immediate and pleasurable connection with others.

* * *

The contributions of performative gestures, memorials, and particular objects rest in their power to shape self-understanding and the values of those who engage with them. They can attune the participant wordlessly to places and times that bear a different quality. They can break into routine and create a new awareness of where one is and why. They are the source of perceptions as well as emotions. Usually based on a bodily and social activity, they give rise to a combination of emotional cognitions and cognitive emotions where knowing and feeling are mutually supportive with neither one being necessarily more significant or more defective in the promotion of awareness. In other words, they carry all the features of the sacred that can make school meaningful and transformative.

CHAPTER 8

When Sacred Cultures Collide

Sharing a sense of the school as sacred can be a powerful motivator and guide in supporting the school and its mission of nurturing learners to know what they need to know to function as contributing members of a community, who have a strong sense of who they are, their place and their value in society, and who have the skills and confidence needed to be active participants in the world around them. While there are many ways this sacredness can be forgotten or denied, there are also many ways it can be sustained and commemorated in places, times, rituals, memorials, and sacred objects.

Some of the challenges facing the schools today, however, come not only from denying or ignoring the sacred character of the school but from conflicting views about what is taken to be sacred. Opposing viewpoints on the multi-layered nature of gender, race, religion, and politics characterize the diversity of most communities today and since the school reflects the larger society, the tensions and conflicts at large are often played out in the school; that is, schools are staging grounds, sometimes even battlegrounds, where conflicting views meet. If the conflict is met with anger, disrespect, incriminations, irrational position-taking, and dictatorial mandates, the sacred boundary of the school may very well be breached. If, on the other hand, truth claims are evidence-based and addressed sincerely, reasonably, with integrity and a view to consensus-building or acceptance and the educational potential of the learners is uppermost, then the sacredness of the school is best protected and empowered in its mission.

There are many instances in schools where conflicting commitments have prevailed without either any attempt at consensus among interested parties or reference to the needs of the current students. One such school stands out as a particularly fraught example of a failed resolution of conflict. It has variously been seen as a test case, a harbinger, a blueprint for other schools, so it is worth a closer look. The students and supporters at New College in Sarasota, Florida, a center for creative learning and a broadly inclusive community since 1960,[215] clashed with moves made by the populist governor in 2023 to realign the school as part of his campaign against what he called "wokism." He replaced college administrators, other school officials, and members of the Board of Trustees with people who shared his objectives while themes of diversity, equity, and inclusiveness (DEI) in the curriculum, student services, and even library books were limited or removed altogether. Some visitors to the campus could not help but notice, and judge, the dress and adornments worn by many of the students that spoke of lifestyles and interests that were different from those often found outside of the college and were perceived as evidence that change was needed. What had been known as a premier honors college was to be re-centered around an athletics program promoted by scholarships, free computers, new residence halls, and plans to build state-of-the-art playing fields and sports facilities to accommodate them, along with an education in Western classics.[216] The governor had easily won re-election and the majority in the state supported his efforts.

However, there was also strong local resistance to these changes. Decisions on tenure were delayed and new rules governing unions passed by the state made it difficult for faculty to bring collective action against these moves. There were, however, *rituals of protest* in many forms. Almost every week there were one or two items in the local paper written mostly by supporters of the old version of the college. Parents and friends attending commencement at the end of the spring semester stood with their backs to the new dignitaries while some seniors staged their own graduation off-campus. At one low point, a student spat on the shoe of one of the most outspoken new trustees. She was given the choice of being charged with assault or leaving the college. The resisting forces, in efforts to preserve their hallowed values, employed protests, advocacy through the media, lawsuits, and debates in meetings with the new trustees. Altogether, the rituals of protest were employed and took many forms.

As I listened to the speeches by the students at their first major public protest, I was impressed by how well they articulated and expressed the values of their besieged college, at how united they were, and how feelingful and yet how wisely they organized and staged their protest. Not only were they trying to educate the general public and the state politicians, but by engaging in the protest they were unifying the student body while clarifying their values and deepening their commitment to them. Although the college remained bent on pursuing the governor's agenda, the protests were not in vain when considering the impact of the protest rituals on the student participants.

A year after the first moves to reinvent the institution were in place, U.S. News and World Report rankings of liberal arts colleges showed a significant drop for New College. There was a significant drop also in gifts from alumni. On the other hand, the administration could boast growing enrollments of new students (even though the total enrollement was largely offset by high rates of attrition), a largely new and energized faculty, a curriculum for freshmen that mostly avoided DEI studies but included discussions around a classic in the Western tradition, *Odysseus*, and plans in development for more studies in technology and professional preparation with links to local commercial interests for work-study experience, and a sounder financial prospect with state funds going to residence hall refurbishment, securing land, and building athletic facilities. While there seemed to be more talk about some items than action around them, the future direction of the college was set and administrators touted developments.

The conflict at the college exposed a typical and opposing sets of sacred values. On the conservative side, the values of a classical, traditional education that centers on canonical Western and often Christian works combined with professional studies to prepare students for the workforce, had to be sustained against perceived erosions by softer, newer, and disturbing studies into race, ethnicity, and gender. The exposure of the spectrum of gender differences in society and the ignored history of slavery and its aftereffect on Black lives with an underlying theme of bringing about social change, for instance, had been central studies in the curriculum and were seen to be not only excessively dominant in what students studied, but also as threats against sacrosanct images of meritocracy, national pride, Western heritage, and traditional family values. The inviolate nature of these beliefs was bolstered further for some by a deep commitment to what are seen as unquestioned biblical fundamentals. Most of the new athletic coaches at New College, for instance, were recruited from fundamentalist Christian schools, in order to help keep the faith.

On the liberal side of the conflict, generations of professors have held to be sacred notions such as academic freedom, university control of the curriculum, free speech, faculty shared-governance, tenure, truth-seeking, experiential learning, along with feminism, civil rights, LGBTQ+ rights, globalization—tenets that were meant to protect the academic program from the very kinds of pressure now being applied. To complicate the issue, some revered values, such as freedom, patriotism, and democracy, are shared by both conservative and liberal parties but how these notions are understood and lived out in practice are also hotly contested.

The conservative forces in this debate at New College did not apply rituals for change against the former program at the college: with state mandates, those with power simply declared there would be change and brought to bear directives, hand-picked appointments to leadership and decision-making positions, and funding to underwrite the changes. Entrenched positions by either side and the absolutist takeover by the "anti-woke" (as they liked to be known) adherents left little room for honest and critical review of the notions and fundamentals both sides held sacred. Actions on the part of the state authorities were sudden and far more dramatically different than what was expected, so that there was little to no time for serious conversations and dialogue among the parties involved. Under these conditions, negotiation, compromise, and cooperation were impossible and antagonism remains between the supporters of the original New College and its new administration.

Consequently, many students and faculty members looked for alternative ways to conduct their teaching and learning and their lives in harmony with their commitments. Some faculty members withdrew completely or took early retirement from what they had come to regard as a hostile and desecrating environment; over a third did not return in the new school year. Many students enrolled in a similar college in another state to complete their studies along the lines they had chosen and in an environment that was more open to their ideals; the attrition rate for returning students was the highest on record. A former chair of the Board of Trustees launched a series of online courses pitched at New College students to give them access to the kinds of studies that had been removed from the curriculum. These courses were fully accredited and could be used to round out degree requirements.[217] When the power and financial resources lie in the hands of one side of a conflict that refuses to negotiate, an impasse has been created. In times of growing authoritarianism, this is more common than one would like to imagine even in democratically based societies. Yet there are still pathways to action.

Even though an outlook may be gloomy, Portuguese writer/journalist Pedro Adão e Silva reminds us that "even pessimism has an auspicious future" for "there is an exuberant and necessary pessimism that dreams of the future"—"an active pessimism, organized, and for now, wholly dedicated to preventing the worst from coming."[218] While one side of a debate may have an upper hand at a point in time, the other is still an important participant, even as a corrective and critic of the other.

When all else fails, even a proactive and plain-spoken withdrawal can be a *ritual of resistance*. This may seem to be claiming too much in the name of ritual to propose that the choices to stay on or to go elsewhere were rituals but, with reference to Collins' theory of interactive rituals,[219] these actions were socially embedded and physically enacted, with a shared emotional mood, sharply focused on values and commitments, and boasting clear boundaries around those against the changes *versus* those for the changes.

As well, for those leaving, a *ritual of farewell* could include opportunities to reflect on the decision while appreciating the educational opportunities up to the time of leaving or mourning the loss of what was most significant in the experience and what those departing would take with and within themselves. Such a gesture could help to assuage some of the anger and disappointment these students were feeling and fortify their determination to move on. Some senior students decided to stay, although there were some early reports that some of them were being harassed by the incoming athlete freshmen. *Rituals of support* for those who chose to stay could be times of reflection on events, planning for ongoing resistance, identifying a community of maintenance and validation, and strategizing how to remain safe and courageous in the face of daunting circumstances. In many situations, rituals of resistance may need to be sustained over a long time.

There are occasions when defeat simply has to be recognized.[220] At New College, the two opposing positions were irreconcilable. The newly empowered conservative side of the conflict accused the other of engaging in "identity politics"; that is, making issues around diverse identities central to the curriculum and organization of the college. It pointed to the fact that over half of the faculty were listed as teachers in the DEI program and most students regardless of their field of study would encounter such courses in their studies. (At first appearance, this may seem very much like an imbalance in the curriculum, but in reality, the DEI program had only one full-time faculty member. Other faculty members were listed in the department because they were willing to offer an occasional course within their discipline area—history, language, literature, philosophy, biology, for instance—that included themes of diversity.) Appointments to faculty required commitment to these values and both in the curriculum and in extracurricular events, diversity issues had been explored and celebrated but were no longer.

When these pervasive positions were rooted out and replaced, those who took a more liberal stance labeled the other as following a "cancel culture" agenda; that is, ignoring, disempowering, and making the different other invisible.[221] At one iconic time, a trailer load of books supporting DEI studies was removed from the library and offered free to any who might want them before the rest would be taken to the dump. A month-long course, entitled "The 'Woke' Movement" was introduced in the 2024–25 school year. Its purpose was to explore "wokeness" through a study of literatures and ideas from both "woke" and "anti-woke" representatives as an introduction to an independent study project on the topic. The course cast wokeness as illiberal in that it resists dissent—a criticism that too often may carry some legitimacy. But the introduction to the course went even further by describing what is called wokeness as a "cult" and asserted that, "Even though they are capable of the most horrendous dehumanising behavior, they think they are the 'good guys.'"[222] (One might ask whether DEI supporters have used similar pejoratives in making moral judgments about conservative positions.) The labels, "identity politics" and "cancel culture" are heavily laden with ethical overtones deepening the rift between the two. In such circumstances, there is no room for negotiation or compromise or even coexistence.

Asking the Right Questions

In these kinds of circumstances, when opposing parties seem to be entrenched, and partisanship locks people into their own ecosphere,[223] a philosophy of education around the sacred can offer some suggestions for a way forward. These may be only partial and thoroughly dependent on the local context and the nature of the conflict and the adherents on both sides, but they may offer some lines to follow toward a resolution.

Typical of a philosophical approach, we begin with asking the right kinds of questions, but this particular philosophy is also influenced by the meaningful consideration of social interaction and embodiment. So, although these questions may seem academic, they are not addressed in the abstract. They are attended to, again as Collins' theory implies, when people come together bodily and face-to-face, focus on answering them, share a passion for the good of the learner and the larger community, and for problem-solving, and exclude extraneous distractions like remembered past insults, the din of outside voices, and unnamed fears.[224] Addressing these questions systematically, critically, and honestly may go some way toward avoiding or dealing with a crisis. The process can begin with identifying and evaluating what opposing parties consider sacred.

Why is this particular sacred commitment, action, concept, or object important to me?

This is an exercise in critical self-evaluation for all participants. It is a matter of naming our passion, weighing its possibilities, assessing its consequences, and being realistic about its limitations. Exposing our sacred beliefs to our critical review may reveal some astonishing features. We may very well discover that some elements of our belief system rest on weak assumptions and need to be replaced or revised. Examining and acknowledging the respective roles of both fact and metaphor, tradition, and myth may bring to light where the legitimate foundations of our beliefs lie. Some parts of the belief structure may have gaps and blind spots. It can be a humbling experience. On the other hand, coming out of such a review, our sacred commitments and values may be stronger, more defensible, and more convincing to us. The time spent in this exercise can also be a celebration of what we collectively hold as sacred within our hearts.

Being clear about what we take to be sacred and what that means in practice prepares us best for sharing with others. When body, mind, and soul are properly aligned around the sacred, articulation and communication of our passion can be most effective and productive, laying the way for dialogue with others. We need not only to explain ourselves but to be open to what others share with us. Feelings can run high but need to be expressed in thoughtful action and reaction, recognizing that different others might also be passionate about their commitments. An exercise in dialogue is not necessarily aimed at changing minds but at least opening understanding between opposing sides.

How can we best practice the values that arise from our commitments?

This is an obvious next step; it basically requires answering the question, So what? Values by nature are powerful yet can be rather ambiguous when translated into specific practice. Sifting and sorting priorities and implications when sacred values serve as guides to practice are important considerations. As a step in resolving an immediate conflict, this question needs to be answered in the context of supporting the school and all its learners at this particular moment. Dialogue around the non-negotiable fundamentals might reveal where options or exceptions can be offered so that some may choose to opt out of a course or an activity or find an alternative when they believe they should not participate.

To what extent should others also accept what we consider sacred?

The answer to this question will be influenced in part by the mission of the particular school. In choosing to affiliate with a school, one chooses to accept its mission and even commits oneself to strengthening that mission and finding ways to live out its vision in critical ways, thus ensuring a measure of uniformity among stakeholders. Such a school would be a "consensus-based community," one in which there is agreement. Admittedly, such a community also tends to "suppress discussion and difference of opinion," "functioning in a relatively authoritarian manner."[225]

A body of scholars can also function as a consensus-based community. Some theoretical foundations and lines of inquiry are favored while those perceived as different can be isolated or ignored. Schools of thought can be faddish, accepted uncritically and allowed not only to dominate the scholarly conversation but also to exclude and disparage alternative viewpoints that might indeed be legitimate. Lauren Kapalka Richerme makes the point that gatekeeping practices, such as reviews for tenure and publication that are intended to protect the integrity of scholarship, can unwittingly preserve prevailing assumptions in the profession by reviewers evaluating others within their own field of vision.[226]

The dialogue between Øivind Varkøy and Petter Dyndahl, "Do We All Have to be 'Leftists,'" reminds us that educators and educational researchers also present as a consensus-based group by tending to be more leftist. In fact, they may in fact be more leftist than those they teach. That is, teachers are more likely to identify with the ideals of a "cultural elite"—educated, cultured, well endowed, progressive—in a time of "dramatic political shifts" and the "breakthrough of populism."[227] The communities school serve may in fact be more right-leaning—suspicious of education, different others, and government institutions including the schools, for example. Reproached for identity politics, educators are not going to compromise their liberal values of DEI while the larger community will continue to censure and remove where possible critical race theory, transgender rights, immigration policies, and other similar themes identified with the so-called cancel culture.

The impasse is not necessarily overcome by either side of the divide assuming tolerance for the other. Built into tolerance is its own undoing: the paradox of tolerance is that by tolerating different viewpoints it inevitably has to tolerate intolerance which can eventually overwhelm it.[228] When right-leaning adherents claim to tolerate the left, they put themselves in the unfortunate position of tolerating the left's intolerance of their tolerance and vice versa, predicting a path of mutual disdain and negation. A similar paradox arises around the notion of inclusion. A stand for inclusion of all has to include those who discriminate and thus opens itself to being discriminated against to the point of obliteration. Moreover, tolerance and inclusion carry the gloss of superiority; they suggest that we acknowledge that the other may be tolerated or not discriminated against even though its adherents are really wrong-headed, unlike "we" who are right.

Varkøy and Dyndahl find a way of moving away from inaction over, although not a resolution of, irreconcilable differences by calling on the writings of Chantal Mouffe. Mouffe proposes that an *antagonistic* approach, argumentative and hostile, dehumanizes the partisan other, where moral judgments are made and opponents become enemies. An *agonistic* approach, strained and confrontational and as noted above pessimistic, in contrast, nevertheless respects the other while admitting fundamental disagreement between them. Both partners behave in a way that recognizes there is no room for compromise while allowing the other to be. They disagree and refuse to accept the others' claims and see the ground between them as contested[229] and that becomes the field of action. Varkøy and Hanne Rinholm, in a later article on the same theme, regard this contested area as the place for critical self-reflection and dialogue. They recommend that discussion and dialogue between parties should not be closed down but pursued vigorously.[230]

In *School Was Our Home*, Martin recalls an unpleasant series of incidents between the Little Red School House students and those from the local public school that illustrates this approach. These public-school "tough eggs," as they became known, and Martin and her classmates were different in fundamental ways—economically, socially, educationally. The public-school students called the Little Red students nasty names, spat, and threw things and harassed them as they moved to and from school; the Little Red students were inclined to flee the scene. There was no room for rapprochement. In its own way, this experience was a small replica of the larger cultural wars that divide schools today. Martin describes the guidance one of her teachers gave them. She had them engage in a "full-fledged" discussion of bullying. Together they proposed a "middle-way solution." They were encouraged to stop, think, and look for this middle-way: it was a matter of "finding a solution between acting as an aggressor or walking away as if nothing were wrong."[231] They were working toward finding an agonistic stance.

What can we do together that is founded on a common sacred value?

Even when compromise on critical issues is impossible in the most divided communities, there is much more that can bring people together than separate them regardless of ideology. Common ground can be found in a shared sense of the sacredness of school and from that, some of its symbols can be embraced by many if not by all. Thresholds symbolizing entry to learning and wisdom, inner sancta where learners with similar interests gather, graduation ceremonies and school openings, sports festivals and trophy cases, for instance, are not the provenance of one side or the other alone but are generally esteemed by all. When community members of all political and religious and ethnic stripes work together with learners and teachers, they can uphold and support the hallowed halls of learning around these shared emblems and in doing so, differences and conflicts can be forgotten for the time. If the entry way is uninviting or shabby or easily ignored, parents and friends can work together to paint it or plant a garden pathway to it. If the computer lab is short on hardware or software, the community can seek out donated equipment. If everyone attends the game and cheers on the local team, it does not matter whether they are liberal or conservative, left-leaning or right, they are contributing to the players' self-understanding and self-esteem, whether they win or lose the match. If they form teams to help teach struggling students how to read, it does not matter what their ideology is. If they provide work-study opportunities for high school and college students, the focus is not on their differences but the job at hand. Working together will not overcome the divide or resolve a conflict, but it can soften the acrimony and raise the level of satisfaction and joy that comes from giving time and energy in service to the school and its learners.

Defending the Idea of the Sacred

An immediate pushback to re-envisioning the school as sacred can arise from very practical reasons. It can be argued that by and large we have the schools that we have and are not usually able to redesign them with new architectural features, specially demarcated boundaries, inner sancta, or labyrinthine portals. The schedule of school days, terms, and years is mandated by departments of education and tradition has set the place, time, and activities around convocations, commencements, and other school rituals. The curriculum is similarly locked in.

However, the lack of sacred geography in the design and layout of a particular school building and timetables that are pre-filled with activities are probably of lesser ultimate consequence than how the places and times of school and topics in the curriculum are regarded. While symbols are vital in constructing space, time, and action, and should be carefully considered and incorporated, they are signifiers; they are not what is symbolized or signified. And so to the school: how one considers the school, what remnants of memory color how one constructs the meaning of the school, and what lingering symbols inform one's conception of places and times where mysteries are revealed, these all are more important than what the physical plant and the schedule of events actually predetermine. The architecture, design, layout, and geography of a sacred place and the interruptions in life paced by metronomic time are attempts to convey the sacred. Regarding the school metaphorically as a sacred place, conducting the most important moments of learning as times of surprise and joy are more significant than any literal space and time.

This does no harm to the notion of the sacred and in fact may be truer to it in some senses. Taking care of the spaces, times, and rituals of a school is being a caretaker of the prompts, the catalysts, the reminders, the inducements to living out the sacred nature of school. To surround a school with a community of support is represented by any perimeter fence; to step inside a school building with a sense of reverence for the role of the educator as guide of the young is why we would hire an architect to design an imposing front door to a school. To develop lesson plans that connect students with significant patterns of meaning in ways that arouse awe and wonder and a commitment to living out the implications of what is learned is why we empower them with furnishings in the inner sanctum of the school with the latest technology and other devices for learning. There is plenty here for teachers, policy makers, parents, and friends of schools to think about, model, and treasure.

At a fundamental level, opposition to the model of the sacredness of school may come from a lingering resistance to the very notion of the sacred itself. Anything that smacks of a religious flavor can draw ire from very different sources. Our age is characterized by secularization: mainline Christian churches, religious orders, and the number of observant believers is dwindling. Talk that borrows from or even hints at religion can be dismissed. At the same time, fundamentalist religious beliefs are growing stronger, evident by the number of mega-churches appearing in cities and towns across the United States and more importantly by the rise of Christian Nationalism which declares that the country is "rightfully Christian and the government should take steps to keep it that way,[232] too often manifest in antisemitism and the desecration of Jewish synagogues and cemeteries. These religious antagonisms are rightfully feared. Meanwhile, Islam is the fastest growing religion in the world and brought to the West increasingly by waves of immigrants, who are seen as a threat by nationalists. When religious commitment is deep-seated and axiomatic, anything religionesque can be suspected. As a consequence, there are those for whom the very idea of the school being sacred runs too close to some religious formulation or other and should be rejected.

There may also be persistent resistance to the idea of a non-religious institution aggregating to itself some of the most important distinguishing features of religion, even at a symbolic level. It may strike some that this effort trivializes, diminishes, or at least misappropriates the things that religions hold dear. However, the church, mosque, temple, or holy mountain top is sacred in a different way than the school. Religious holy places are dedicated to worship and building religious faith in believers; schools are dedicated to education and building knowledge and understanding in students. Both kinds of settings can be consecrated for their high value and purpose and certainly the schools can be mythologized and dedicated as sacred places for the sacred is not possessed by religion alone.

Two considerations are relevant here. First, one cannot make something that is not normally regarded as religious sanctified by fiat. We simply do not have full control over what is and is not sacred. As Eliade explains, the sacred appears as a hierophany, a breakthrough of the sacred into the secular, and it is that which consecrates a place. As he says, "The place is never 'chosen' by man; it is merely discovered by him; ... the sacred place in some way or another reveals itself to him."[233]

Second, if we trace the tradition of education, we are reminded that schools were in the main founded by religions. Priests, theologians, imams, rabbis, and shamans were the original teachers, and the curriculum was designed to support the faith. Learning and faith, theology and science, knowledge and inspiration, mind and soul were not opposites in tension but worked together just as cognition depends on emotion and bodily reactions give rise to feelings and understanding. To recapture some of this original intent in the sense of the sacred purposes and missions of the schools seems to be not such a big step away from education's origins. Our references to "the hallowed halls of learning" echo this past in our present metaphors, and the rituals of convocation and commencement, for instance, re-call a very old consecration of teachers and students to their sacred callings, dressed in traditional robes, mortar boards, and stoles. In other words, while it may not be within our power to declare a space and time and gesture sacred, it may be quite within our reach to remember that school space has always been sacred, and we are simply revivifying that notion. As Whitehead claimed, the essence of education is that it be religious, that is, it is about life and how to live it.

Holding the sacred and secular apart in one's experience makes for a fragmented way of living and is a phenomenon that particularly marks the modern Western mind. For many across times and cultures, the sacred has a way of overflowing its boundaries so that its surroundings and all the activities around it are touched and elevated to sacrality. Trying to contain the sacred within some defined space does not so much protect it as limit and disempower it. Teachers and administrators who have a finely tuned sense of the sacred will carry that sensitivity into all their dealings with family, vocation, and business and it will influence their work within the school. The presence of the sacred is a testament to its power and exemplified in institutions that serve to elevate the community by protecting its young and opening to them the mysteries of the world around them.

Remembering this may reinvigorate the public imagination about the true role and purpose of the school. If the sacred is evident in transformational learning, breakthroughs to new meaning, a growing awareness of the world and one's place within it, and a sense of calling and value, then these possibilities should occupy our minds as scholars, curriculum builders, policy makers, administrators, and classroom teachers. If we attend to the elements that mark a space and time as sacred, symbolically if not literally, we can reinforce our endeavors, and the overall impact will contribute to making our places of learning places of great power as well.

* * *

There is no quick and easy way to resolve conflict when sacred ideals clash. In fact, there may be no resolution at all. But drawing on shared sacred symbols and commitment to the overarching sense that school is sacred can go some way to maintaining an environment that puts the student learner central. Honestly asking the right kinds of questions of ourselves, enacting the answers with rituals of change or protest or grieving or agonizing, and finding common cause in shared projects can ameliorate and possibly disrupt suspicion and hostility on school campuses when a struggle arises. Above all, holding fast to the notion that school is sacred inspires, empowers, and guides the teachers and learners, and the communities that sustain them. Against such a backdrop, we can look at the problems and solutions faced by schools today, evaluate them, and possibly find a way to address them. We have principles to guide our decisions and actions.

CHAPTER 9

Reflections

A philosophy of education analyzes, untangles, clarifies, and critically reflects on ideas and theories and truth claims but its conclusions are also measured and tested in the world of practice. We can expect such a philosophy to offer some principles to guide us when we contemplate our particular role in the school, whether it be within the walls of the building or in the surrounding community. We will explore some suggestions that might emerge when the lens of the sacred is applied by the stakeholders to the project of education

When *parents and community supporters* see the school as sacred, they can re-evaluate the role of the school in their own lives and the lives of those following them. One cannot but recall the story of the of the reluctant teacher appointed to the remote school in Bhutan as told in *Lunana: A Yak in the Classroom*. The whole village set out across the mountains and valleys to meet the teacher as he trekked toward his new appointment. The moment when he lifts his eyes and sees the villagers lined along the rim of a hill to greet him is moving and inspiring.[234] This moment also shares a similar dynamic with the Tongan mothers who gathered in a circle under the trees near the school when the visitors came to check on how the school was doing. They were so filled with pride and joy in their school, and they waited for affirmation.[235] The children in these communities will flourish. Parents and neighbors everywhere can seek ways to provide the school with the resources it needs to fulfill its role. They can uphold the efforts of the teachers for their children and young people with understanding and high regard, while recognizing that these classroom heroes are human and imperfect. In their actions and reactions to the efforts of the school they can seek dialogue with a view to cooperating and negotiating with respect and an open mind and a clear voice.

When *local officials and civic administrators* see the school through the lens of the sacred, they may take into greater account the symbolic meaning of elements of the architecture of the school during a new building or renovation program. They may consider how to maximize or at least capture the significance of the fence, entryway and threshold, windows, classroom layout and design, furniture choices, and the embellishments in specialized rooms and spaces. They can imagine groups of learners gathered in the computer lab, art studio, home room, science lab, or sports field coming alive with the prospect of learning, discovering, and finding their joy.

They will also enact policies to make the school free from violence from within and without; they can promote laws to keep guns out of the hands of the disturbed and/or underaged, and high-capacity assault rifles out of the hands of everybody. Such are the dangerous times in which we live, they may instruct teachers and staff and the students how to be safe if danger comes to the classroom or the playground. They can put in place clear response procedures and train personnel in how to respond to emergencies or perceived threats or warning signs.

In a similar vein, they can also expect that the expression of ideas and emotions be free and at the same time civil and open to critique in the school space. They will ensure as did the teachers at the Little Red School House[236] and in the *Casa dei Bambini* of Montessori's classrooms,[237] opportunities to not only learn content but self-understanding. Policies and attitudes toward the diversity of students who make up a school community need to be articulated and enforced to protect every learner from discrimination and harassment and nurture their growth authentically.

When *school leaders* see the school through the lens of the sacred, they may be compelled to guard the perimeters, thresholds, and inner sancta of the school and also its sacred objects and memorials. They can employ the variety of ways that teachers know so well—modeling, attending, informing—to lead the school community to understand the deeper significance of these things. That is also true of the celebrations, festivities, openings and closings of school times. Beginning the school year with a convocation is accompanied by a sense of a fresh start and renewed motivation. Closing a school year with a graduation or even a simple event like the one I witnessed at a local school where the teachers and staff gathered on the lawn and waved goodbye to their students for the summer break as the children waved back,[238] can make school and what it endeavors to accomplish special in the minds of participants.

These occasions and events can contribute in ways not always as well conveyed in words, as it did for me in the flag-raising ceremony at my school. I became a part of a much bigger community and my place in the world reached out toward new boundaries.[239] The flag could not continue to do that for me as I increasingly came to appreciate its exclusions and limitations but as I grew, my ceremonies and rituals also grew and so did the world in which I live. That is the way with rituals—they sometimes need to be revisited, reclaimed, or replaced to remain relevant.

Down times and quiet zones can be planned; a break in the monotony of the ticking clock, a change in routine, taking learning to a different setting by a school excursion, for instance, can help a learner see the world with new eyes. If the school building is decrepit and in a poor neighborhood, leaders can still nurture what there is of the sense of the sacred: discovering a life of meaning wherever one is. With some proactive plans for renovation, the school, as a sacred center, may even become a nucleus for neighborhood renewal. If the school is well endowed, those in charge may point beyond the material assets of the school to the true meaning of learning and the responsibilities that are entailed. As a further outcome, the learners and their supporters may seek out ways to share the resources more equitably with learners in other neighborhoods.

When *curriculum designers and lesson planners* see the school through the lens of the sacred, they can be encouraged to acknowledge the potential of giving the learners not only more knowledge, but also more self-understanding, awe, wonder, joy, and hope. The content of learning is more than facts, information, and rote learning. It is a series of mysteries to be explored. We can recall JoJo, the kindergartner in Auvergne, France who glimpsed infinity as he was learning that counting by numbers seemed to come to no end.[240] When I heard the grade above me was learning how to do long division, I too was enthralled with the mystery of this mathematical maneuver. It so captured my imagination, I too wanted to be admitted into this mystery.[241] In my own way it was not dissimilar from Ursula Goodenough's encounter with the mystery of the universe as a student of physics. When she saw the stars from her sleeping bag on a camping trip, she was so overwhelmed with the inevitable pointlessness of it all, she buried her head. But she has come to accept with some calmness the inscrutability of the universe as a wondrous given.[242] In encounters with the unknown that an education affords, the learner transcends her smaller world and the sacred is manifest.

Curriculum designers can build in opportunities for the learning to deviate from the meeting of information and skill objectives to encountering the personal meaning that lies within that information. A well-placed and non-threatening question or moment of reflection built into the schedule is not a waste of time. When the children at the Little Red School House, for instance, were being bullied by the neighborhood "bad eggs," their teacher chose to stop work and lead a discussion about how they might find a way that did not lead to more aggression, but at the same time, did not give way to fright and flight.[243] That model for approaching a losing battle was one that could influence a lifetime of behavior in the face of conflict. Studies in music and the other arts, literature, honest inquiries into history, gender, and ethnic studies, and the scientific exploration of the wonders of the world we occupy can be transformative when they transcend the facts in search of personal meaning.

When *teachers, their teaching aides, and their supervisors* see the school through the lens of the sacred, they can glimpse just how high and deep their calling is. It might feel both overwhelming (*tremendum*) and irresistible (*fascinans*) at the same time. This is in part because they are called on to draw those same feelings out of what they are called to teach, opening up this potential for their students. In the daily tasks of teaching, they may not always sense the impact their work is having on the lives of their students. I did not expect the student in my service-learning course to undergo such shock and surprise when she found her homeless shelter resident turn away from an opportunity to win back her children from foster homes. Nor did I predict that the student would find in this moment a life-changing event that would lead her into a career in family services.[244] Teachers can be satisfied when their efforts result in an active learning environment and when there are quiet lulls for reflection. They can see the motivational power of introducing their learners to where in the schedule or the curriculum they can find their center, their self, collectively and individually. They can resist moves that would take away their academic freedom in the classroom and in their research knowing their calling is sacred.

When *learners* see the school through the lens of the sacred, they may be motivated to seek the moments of enlightenment. They can choose to put aside the distractions of their electronic devices to make room in their attending hearts and minds to discover the indescribable. They cannot be afraid of learning something so new it calls into question the edifice of their understanding up to that point. They can rise to the challenge of mastering a new skill or exceeding their personal best for that is an important avenue to joy and surprise. They can learn from their studies as well as from their teachers and friends, especially the different others with whom they share the classroom. They can choose their heroes wisely, making those choices on the basis of what is of greatest value. They will not be afraid to question in search of meaning and defining their values.

A sense of the sacredness of education endows learners with a measure of permission to seek out and protect and celebrate the learnings that give them meaning and purpose. As we learned earlier, Lon, the first grader, discovered this in his violin lessons which ostensibly changed him from "a complete hellion." into "a complete angel." When his lessons were threatened in second grade, he let his school know how he felt about the loss in no uncertain terms.[245] The high schoolers, who built their community and sense of self on the bat-tennis court, kept the memory alive even to a mythic level, when renovators tore the court apart.[246] The college students who were gaining deeper understandings of themselves through their literature studies and poetry writing, created a ritual, Naked Poetry Reading, to express and honor this.[247] The students at New College, who staged protests of various kinds in an attempt to save the kinds of studies in diversity and social change that had been at the heart of the curriculum they had signed up for, were not only articulating their beliefs but deepening them.[248] Learners can lay claim to what is sacred for them and the school can be alert to giving them the freedom to do so.

Opening oneself to the sacred nature of the school is an invitation to see learning in its wholeness. At its heart, education is not a turning away but an invitation to join in. When next we come upon the entryway to a school building, we may see it as more than just a door; we may imagine it as a portal to understanding and wisdom. When we see a learner daydreaming, we may regard that moment as more than a waste of time; but instead encourage it as potentially a moment of meaning-making. When we arrive at the beginning of a new school term, we may consider it as more than just another festive ritual; we may celebrate it as the beginning of a new phase of growth toward knowing and understanding. When we consider a student, grappling with assignments, deadlines, projects, and examinations, we may observe here something more than a student to be filled with information and knowledge; we may realize that here is a learner on the way toward increasing levels of understanding and deeper dimensions of wisdom if we help point the way. With the lens of sacredness, we have a more fulsome image of the school and the learners who occupy it.

Notes

1 *Lunana: A Yak in the Classroom*, director Pawo Choyning Dorji, Samuel Goldwyn Films, 2019.

2 Plato, *Apology*, 38a5–6.

3 Nelson Goodman, *Ways of Worldmaking* (Indianapolis, IN: Hackett Publishing Co., 1978).

4 For an analysis of a number of models, see Estelle R. Jorgensen, *Pictures of Music Education* (Bloomington, Indiana: Indiana University Press, 2011). She discusses the "factory" model (91–110) and the "garden" model (111–130), looking at each model from the perspective of the teacher, administrator, and curriculum builder. Although her examples are drawn from music education, the ideas are applicable to other areas of the curriculum.

5 John Amos Comenius, *The Great Didactic*, trans M. W. Keatinge (Whitefish, MT: Kessinger Publishing, 1910), 281–282.

6 Mircea Eliade, *Myth and Reality*, trans Willard R. Trask (NY: Harper Colophon Books, 1963), 162–193.

7 Alfred North Whitehead, *The Aims of Education and Other Essays* (New York: Free Press, 1929), 14.

8 Whitehead, *The Aims of Education*, 2.

9 Whitehead, *The Aims of Education*, 6–7.

10 Whitehead, *The Aims of Education*, 12.

11 <https://www.britannica.com/event/Dunblane-school-massacre>.

12 <https://www.britannica.com/event/Beslan-school-attack>.

13 <https://people.com/crime/thailand-kindergarten-mass-shooting-death-toll/>.

14 <https://en.wikipedia.org/wiki/List_of_school_shootings_in_the_United_States>, accessed Jan 28, 2022.

15 In the Parkland, Florida school shooting in 2019, several police officers resigned, and the sheriff was removed from office for staying outside the school and failing to confront the shooter. In 2024, the U.S. Department of Justice released a 500-page report on the response of police and other emergency responders to the shooting at Uvalde, Texas which claimed the lives of 19 children and two teachers in 2022. The report details the lack of competence and leadership which left the children unprotected with the shooter in the classroom for over an hour. <https://drive.google.com/file/d/1pPFA4GsYIDkxj3xe_fpO-WdCdtfp2bb2/view>.

16 See for instance, "School Board Targets Comments, *Sarasota Herald-Tribune/ US Today Network*, January 23, 2022, 1A, 3A.

17 A scathing report was issued by the American Association of University Professors in 2023, "Report of a Special Committee: Political Interference and Academic Freedom in Florida's Public Higher Education System," <https://www.aaup.org/report/report-special-committee-political-interference-and-academic-freedom-florida%E2%80%99s-public-higher>. It not only describes what is happening in one state but situates these events in the wider context of the US. Already the report is out of date in the sense that the movements described in Florida are spreading quickly through other conservative states. These developments are not restricted to the United States or the western world but appear elsewhere as well; see, for instance, "'It is Suffocating': A Top Liberal University in Under Attack in India," *New York Times*, Feb 12, 2024, section A1 <https://www.nytimes.com/2024/02/10/world/asia/india-bjp-jnu.html?searchResultPosition=1>.

18 Monika Stachowiak-Kudła, Sina Westa, Catarina Santos Botelho, Ildikó Bartha, Academic Freedom as a Defensive Right, *Hague Journal on the Rule of Law*, 15 (2023): 161–190. <https://doi.org/10.1007/s40803-022-00188-4>. Evelien Timbermont, "Academic Freedom as a Fundamental Feature of Academia: A European Union Perspective," *Higher Education Policy* 36 no.2 (2023): 394–410. <https://doi.org/10.1057/s41307-021-00261-x>. Eva Maria Vögtle and Michael Windzio, "Does Academic Freedom Matter for Global Student Mobility? Results from Longitudinal Network Data 2009–2017," *Higher Education (00181560)* 87, no. 2 (2024)): 433–52. <https://doi.org/10.1007/s10734-023-01015-x>. In the US, a statement of the principle of academic freedom was first announced in 1915 and since then the original statement has been revisited and refined. The standard iteration by the Association of University Professors was in 1940. <https://www.aaup.org/report/1940-statement-principles-academic-freedom-and-tenure>.

19 American Association of University Professors, "1940 Statement of Principles on Academic Freedom and Tenure, with 1970 Interpretive Comments," 14. <https://www.aaup.org/file/1940%20Statement.pdf>.

20 American Association of University Professors, "Statement of Principles on Academic Freedom and Tenure," 1940. <https://www.aaup.org/report/1940-statement-principles-academic-freedom-and-tenure>.

21 Kenneth Stern, "Academic Freedom, Boycotts, Definitions, and Democracy," *University of the Pacific Law Review* 54, no 4 (2023): 716–20. <https://search.ebscohost.com/login.aspx?>.

22 Balch, "Is Academic Freedom in Crisis?"; Ryan Quinn, "Indiana U Board Doubles Down on Protest Restrictions," *Inside Higher Education* (July 30, 2024),

<https://www.insidehighered.com/news/students/free-speech/2024/07/30/indiana-u-board-doubles-down-protest-restrictions?utm_source=Inside+Higher+Ed&utm_campaign=ef846c303e-DNU_2021_COPY_02&utm_medium=email&utm_term=0_1fcbc04421-ef846c303e-238205906&mc_cid=ef846c303e&mc_eid=c2b64506c5>; Anemona Hartocollis, "Professors in Trouble Over Protests Wonder if Academic Freedom Is Dying," *New York Times*, October 23, 2024, <https://www.nytimes.com/2024/10/23/us/faculty-protests-academic-freedom-tenure-discipline.html>.

23 Jonathan Malesic, "There's a Very Good Reason College Students Don't Read Anymore," *New York Times Opinion*, Oct 25, 2024 <https://www.nytimes.com/2024/10/25/opinion/college-university-students-reading.html?smid=em-share>.

24 See for instance, Bridget Balch, "Is Academic Freedom in Crisis?" *Associate of American Medical Colleges News* (Nov 29, 2023). <https://www.aamc.org/news/academic-freedom-crisis>; D. B. Audretsch, C. Fisch, C. Franzoni, P. Momtaz, and S. Vismara, (2024) "Academic Freedom and Innovation," *PLoS ONE* 19 no.6 (2024): e0304560. <https://doi.org/10.1371/journal.pone.0304560>; Ryan Quinn, "A Year of Investigations, Punishments and Arrests of Scholars," *Inside Higher Education*, October 8, 2024 <https://www.insidehighered.com/news/faculty-issues/academic-freedom/2024/10/08/faculty-investigated-punished-arrested-oct-7-2023?utm_source=Inside+Higher+Ed&utm_campaign=3244dde610-DNU_2021_COPY_02&utm_medium=email&utm_term=0_1fcbc04421-3244dde610-238205906&mc_cid=3244dde610&mc_eid=c2b64506c5>.

25 Andrea Cassani, "COVID-19 and the Democracy–Autocracy Freedom Divide: Reflections on Post-Pandemic Regime Change Scenarios." *Political Studies Review*, 20, no 4 (2022): 717–724. <https://doi.org/10.1177/14789299211047087>.

26 Darrell M. West, "Why Academic Freedom Challenges are Dangerous for Democracy," *Brown Center Chalkboard*, Sept 8, 2022. <https://www.brookings.edu/articles/why-academic-freedom-challenges-are-dangerous-for-democracy/COMMENTARY>; Giulio Marini and Anatoly Oleksiyenko, "Academic Freedom in the Re-imagined Post-Humboldtian Europe," *Higher Education Quarterly*, 76 no. 3 (2022): 513–20, <https://doi.org/10.1111/hequ.12405>; Nuraan Davids, "Academic Freedom and the Fallacy of a Post-Truth Era," *Educational Philosophy & Theory*, 53 no.11 (2021)): 1183–93. <https://doi.org/10.1080/00131857.2021.1917363>.

27 Ryan Quinn, "'Don't Miss': Does Academic Freedom Excuse Offensive Posts About Assassination Attempts?" *Inside Higher Education* (July 24, 2024), <https://www.insidehighered.com/news/faculty-issues/academic-freedom/2024/07/24/does-academic-freedom-excuse-posts-assassination>.

28 See, for instance, "1940 Statement of Principles on Academic Freedom and Tenure, 14; K. E. Whittington, "Academic Freedom and the Mission of the University," *Houston Law Review*, 59, no.4 (2022): 821–841.

29 Robin Hackett and Javier Rivera, "Free Speech and Academic Freedom in the Era of the Alt-Right." *Radical Teacher*, no. 118 (Fall, 2020): 31–40. <https://doi.org/10.5195/rt.2020.742>.

30 Iris M. Yob, *For Profit and For Good: Walden University 1970–2020* (Cambridge, UK: Ethics International Press, 2023) 148–49; Ronald D. Simpson, "How Higher Education Differs from Corporate America," *Innovative Higher Education*, 26, no. 4 (Summer, 2002): 231–233.

31 Yob, in *For Profit and for Good*, traces the story of how one for-profit university faced this challenge and sought to resolve it in changing contexts over five decades. In essence, any success of the resolution depended on clarifying roles and mutual and informed cooperation.

32 See, for instance, the report from the National Institute for Health: <https://www.nih.gov/news-events/nih-research-matters/cyberbullying-linked-suicidal-thoughts-attempts-young-adolescents>.

33 Claire Duffy, CNN, "'There are no Guardrails.' This Mom Believes an AI Chatbot is Responsible for her Son's Suicide," <https://www.msn.com/en-us/news/other/there-are-no-guardrails-this-mom-believes-an-ai-chatbot-is-responsible-for-her-son-s-suicide/ar-AA1tbWG1?ocid=BingNewsSerp>.

34 See, for instance, Bianca Barton, Katherine S. Adams, Blaine L. Browne, Meagan C. Arrstia-Chisholm, "The Effects of Social Media Usage on Attention, Motivation, and Academic Performance," *Active Learning in Higher Education*, 22, no.1 (2021): 11–22 <https://doi.org/10.1177/1469787418782817> and Remedios C. Kulidtod and Nahida S. Pasagui, "Effects of Social Networking Media to the Academic Performance of the Students," *Advances in Economics, Business and Management Research*, vol. 45 (2017): 59–64 <www.atlantis-press.com/proceedings/coema-17/25882337>.

35 Noam Chomsky, Ian Roberts and Jeffrey Watumull, "Noam Chomsky: The False Promise of ChatGPT," <https://www.nytimes.com/2023/03/08/opinion/noam-chomsky-chatgpt-ai.html>.

36 The Health, Education, Labor, and Pensions Department of the U.S. Senate launched a study into the practices of for-profit universities and colleges in the country. The final report issued July 30, 2012 and entitled "For Profit Higher Education: The Failure to Safeguard the Federal Investment and Ensure Student Success" reveals many of the unscrupulous maneuvers of these institutions and the erosion of good practices in recruiting, retaining, teaching, and determining tuition. The report also notes that while these shady customs were prevalent, they were not universal and cites other outstanding examples of

properly run institutions that put student success first. See <https://www.help.senate.gov/imo/media/for_profit_report/PartI.pdf>.

37 Elizabeth H. MacGregor, "Conceptualizing Musical Vulnerability," *Philosophy of Music Education Review* 30, no. 1 (Spring 2022): 24–43.

38 Interview with Brenda Brenner, Professor of Violin and Music Education, Indiana University, Jacobs School of Music, February 10, 2014.

39 I am indebted to Cathy Benedict who raised this question in response to my earlier version of Chapter 5, Sacred Time, at the International Society of Philosophy of Music Education conference, Frankfurt, Germany, June 2015.

40 "Sacred." *Merriam-Webster.com Dictionary*, Merriam-Webster, <https://www.merriam-webster.com/dictionary/sacred. Accessed Jan 27, 2022>.

41 Separation of church and state is a phrase that refers to the Establishment Clause of the First Amendment of the U.S. Constitution. The metaphor of a "wall of separation" was introduced by then U.S. president, Thomas Jefferson, in 1802. The phrase has been used repeatedly in Supreme Court decisions since then.

42 For a summary of the legal positions on the question of religious clubs meeting on school grounds see <https://www.rutherford.org/files_images/general/B14_Public-School-Religious-Clubs.pdf>.

43 See for example, <https://www.encyclopedia.com/science/encyclopedias-almanacs-transcripts-and-maps/evolution-and-creationism-american-public-schools>.

44 See for example, <https://www.adl.org/education/resources/tools-and-strategies/religion-in-public-schools/curriculum#:~:text=Public%20schools%20may%20not%20teach%20religion%2C%20although%20teaching,of%20the%20Bible%20as%20a%20religious%20document.%202>.

45 See for example, <https://www.adl.org/education/resources/tools-and-strategies/religion-in-public-schools/dress-codes#:~:text=The%20public%20schools%20generally%20are%20permitted%20to%20accommodate,a%20number%20of%20significant%20exceptions%20to%20this%20rule>.

46 See William Michael Perrine, "*Bauchman v. West High School* Revisited: Religious Text and Context in Music Education," *Philosophy of Music Education Review* 25, no. 2 (2017): 192–213. <https://doi.org/10.2979/philmusieducrevi.25.2.06>; William Perrine, "*In Loco Parentis* and the Politically-Directed Music Curriculum," *Philosophy of Music Education Review* 27, no. 2 (2019): 171–91. <https://doi.org/10.2979/philmusieducrevi.27.2.05>.

47 Random House Kernerman Webster's College Dictionary, 2010 K Dictionaries Ltd. (Random House, Inc 2005, 1997, 1991.

48 Collins Thesaurus of the English Language, Complete and Unabridged 2nd Edition (HarperCollins Publishers 1995, 2002).

49 Sam Keen, *To a Dancing God* (New York: Harper and Row, 1970), 150–157.
50 Massimo Rosati, "The Archaic and Us: Ritual, Myth, the Sacred and Modernity," *Philosophy and Social Criticism* 40, no. 4–5 (2014): 365.
51 I have discussed these experiences in "If We Knew What Spirituality Was, We Would Teach for It," *Music Educators Journal* 98, no. 1 (2011): 41–47.
52 Benjamin S. Bloom, M. D. Engelhart, E. J. Furst, W. H. Hill, and D. R. Krathwohl, *Taxonomy of Educational Objectives: The Classification of Educational Goals* (New York: David McKay Company, 1956).
53 Amanda Williamson, "Reflections and Theoretical Approaches to the Study of Spiritualities within the Field of Somatic Movement Dance Education," *Journal of Dance and Somatic Practices* 2 (2010): 35–61.
54 Keen, *To a Dancing God* develops this theme.
55 Israel Scheffler, *In Praise of the Cognitive Emotions* (New York, London: Routledge, 1991), 4–9.
56 Parker J. Palmer, in *To Know as We are Known: Education as a Spiritual Journey* (San Francisco: Harper, 1993 [1983]), 1–2 raises the dilemma faced by those who created the first atomic bomb.
57 Palmer, *To Know as We are Known*, xxiii.
58 I have explored this proposition before in Iris M. Yob, "Cognitive Emotions and Emotional Cognitions in the Arts," *Journal of Aesthetic Education* 32, no. 2 (Summer, 1978): 27–40. Iris. M. Yob, "Cognitive Emotions and Emotional Cognitions in Religious Studies," *Religion and Education*, 28, No.1 (Spring, 2001): 95–104. The description of emotional cognitions given here is a further development of my thinking about this topic over time.
59 Lynda Sexson, *Ordinarily Sacred* (New York: Crossroad, 1982) explores the notion of finding the sacred in the everyday symbols around us. Her interpretations are given in religious terms but in a revitalized sense.
60 Scheffler, *In Praise of the Cognitive Emotions*, 10–11.
61 Scheffler, *In Praise of the Cognitive Emotions*, 12–15.
62 C. S. Lewis, *Surprised by Joy: The Shape of My Early Life* (London: Collins, 1955 [1976]), 108–111.
63 Even in science, however, one cannot be sure of the immutability of known truths. John Dewey, in *The Quest for Certainty* (Capricorn Books, 1933), argues that in the most rational of scientific enterprises, certain knowledge is illusory because subsequent discoveries can modify or even undermine what is taken as truth.
64 Acts 9:1–9. The story is told that on his way to Damascus to wreak further havoc on the early adherents to the faith espoused by Jesus, carrying letters authorizing their destruction and breathing murderous threats, Saint Paul was suddenly struck down by a bright light from heaven. A voice spoke to him:

"Saul, Saul (for that was his pre-Christian name), why are you persecuting me?" In fact, the light was so bright it blinded him temporarily. His assistants had to lead him to the destination. But at that moment of revelation, he was converted to Christianity and became one of the most significant leaders and theologians of the movement.

65 See for instance, Salwa Khoddam, "The Enclosed Garden in C. S. Lewis' *The Chronicles of Narnia*," 2009, <https://www.cslewis.org/journal/the-enclosed-garden-in-cs-lewis%e2%80%99-the-chronicles-of-narnia/>; Todd Haiman, "Hortus Conclusis," <https://www.toddhaimanlandscapedesign.com/blog/2011/02/hortus-conclusus.html>.

66 Or in the Latin *Fides quaerens intellectum*, a phrase from Anselm, Bishop of Canterbury in the Eleventh Century.

67 C.S. Lewis, *The Pilgrim's Regress; An Allegorical Apology for Christianity, Reason and Romanticism*, 3rd edn. (Great Britian: Collins 1933), Chapter 2 "The Island," 31–34.

68 Lewis, *Surprised by Joy*, 114–120.

69 Social constructionism is a school of thought that can be traced back to Margaret Mead's 1930s book, *Mind, Self and Society*, and to Lev Vygotsky (1896–1934) who has been particularly influential in applying the theory to education. In essence, social constructionism proposes that the social environment and interaction with others contributes to cognitive development.

70 In Vygotsky's own words, the zone of proximal development is "the distance between the actual developmental level as determined by independent problem solving and the level of potential development as determined through problem-solving under adult guidance, or in collaboration with more capable peers" in L. S. Vygotsky, *Mind in Society: The Development of Higher Psychological Processes* (Cambridge, MA: Harvard University Press, 1978), 86.

71 Gilbert Ryle, *The Concept of Mind*, intro. Julia Tanney (Routledge: New York, [1948], 2009). See especially, Chapter 2, "Knowing How and Knowing That." See also an entry in the *Stanford Encyclopedia of Philosophy*, Carlotta Pavese, "Knowledge How," (2021) <https://plato.stanford.edu/entries/knowledge-how/> Both Tanney and Pavese acknowledge the importance of Ryle in undermining dualist theories of mind-body, but in the light of contemporary thinking, Ryle did not go far enough: mind and body in knowing how are one.

72 Among the writers that formed the database for this qualitative study are June Boyce-Tillman, "Promoting Wellbeing through Music Education," *Philosophy of Music Education Review*, 8 (2000): 89–98 and "Spirituality in the Musical Experience," in L. Bresler, ed., *International Handbook of Research in Arts Education* (New York: Springer, 2007), 1405–1422; Deanne Bogdan, "Musical Spirituality: Reflections on Identity and the Ethics of Embodied Aesthetic

Experience in/and the Academy," *Journal of Aesthetic Education*, 32 no. 2 (2003): 80–98 and "The Shiver-Shimmer Factor: Musical Spirituality, Emotion and Education," *Philosophy of Music Education Review*, 18 (2010): 111–129; Wayne Bowman, "Cognition and the Body: Perspectives from Music Education," in L. Bresler, *Knowing Bodies, Moving Minds: Toward Embodied Teaching and Learning* (Dordrecht, the Netherlands: Kluwer, 2004), 29–50; David Carr, "Exploring the Spiritual and Moral Light and Dark Sides of Musical Experience and Appreciation, *Philosophy of Music Education Review*, 18 (2010): 130–144; Anthony Palmer, "Music Education and Spirituality: Philosophical Exploration ll," *Philosophy of Music Education Review*, 14 (2006):143–158 and "Spirituality in Music Education: Transcending Culture, Exploration lll," *Philosophy of Music Education Review*, 18 (2010): 152–170; Iris M. Yob, "Why is Music a Language of Spirituality," *Philosophy of Music Education Review*, 18 (2010): 145–151 and "If We Knew What Spirituality Was We Would Teach for It," *Music Educators Journal*, 98 (2011): 41–47.

73 Max van Manen, *Researching Lived Experience: Human Science for an Action Sensitive Pedagogy* (London, Ontario: Althouse Press, 1998 [2002, 2003]), 101–106.

74 Liesl van der Merwe and John Habron, "A Conceptual Model of Spirituality in Music Education," *Journal of Research in Music Education* 63, no. 1 (2015): 55–56. <https://doi.org/10.1177/0022429415575314>.

75 Deanne Bogdan, The Shiver-Shimmer Factor: Musical Spirituality, Emotion, and Education," *Philosophy of Music Education Review* 18, no, 2 (Fall, 2010): 111–129.

76 See the Biblical story in Exodus 3.

77 Koji Matsunobu, "The Impermanence of All Things," paper presented at the International Society for the Philosophy of Music Education, Oslo, Norway, July 2023.

78 Steve Habelin, "Teaching Spirituality," <https://www.educationworld.com/blog/teaching-spirituality>. He cites G. Claxton, "Mind Expanding: Scientific and Spiritual Foundations for the Schools We Need," paper presented at the Graduate School of Education Public Lectures, University of Bristol, UK, 2002; M. M. Piechowski, "Emotional and Spiritual Giftedness," in N. Colangelo and G. A. Davis, eds., *Handbook of Gifted Education*, 3rd ed. (Boston, MA: Pearson Education 2003); and M. L. Pava, Spirituality in (and out) of the Classroom: A Pragmatic Approach," *Journal of Business Ethics*, 73, no. 3 (2007): 287–299.

79 Van der Merwe and Habron, "A Conceptual Model of Spirituality in Music Education," 47–69. <https://doi.org/10.1177/0022429415575314>.

80 Paul Ricoeur, *Figuring the Sacred: Religion, Narrative, and Imagination*, trans., David Pellauer, ed., Mark I. Wallace (Minneapolis: Fortress Press, 1995), 48–65.

81 Nelson Goodman, *Languages of Art* (Indianapolis, Hackett Publishing Co., 1976), 252.

82 Ricoeur, *Figuring the Sacred*, 51.

83 Howard Gardner, *Frames of Mind: The Theory of Multiple Intelligences* (New York: Basic Books, Inc, 1983).

84 Gardner, *Frames of Mind*, 103.

85 Susanne K. Langer, *Philosophy in a New Key: A Study in the Symbolism of Reason, Rite, and Art*, 3rd edition (Cambridge, MA: Harvard University Press, 1952), 94–96.

86 Brendan Hyde, "Beyond Logic—Entering the Realm of Mystery: Hermeneutic Phenomenology as a Tool for Reflecting on Children's Spirituality," *International Journal of Children's Spirituality* 10, no. 1 (April 2005): 31–44.

87 Langer, *Philosophy in a New Key*, 97.

88 Rudolf Otto, *The Idea of the Holy: An Inquiry into the Non-rational Factor in the Idea of the Divine and its Relation to the Rational*, 2nd edition. trans John W. Harvey (London: Oxford University Press, 1950), 2.

89 Mircea Eliade, *The Sacred and the Profane*, trans Willard R. Trask (San Diego: Harcourt Brace Jovanovich Publishers, 1959), 12.

90 Paul Tillich, *Ultimate Concern: Tillich in Dialogue*, ed. D. McKenzie Brown (New York: Harper and Row, 1965), 11.

91 See also Hyde, "Beyond Logic," 38; van der Merwe and Habron, "A Conceptual Model of Spirituality," 60–62.

92 Ursula Goodenough, *The Sacred Depths of Nature* (New York: Oxford University Press, 1998).

93 See <https://www.merriam-webster.com/dictionary/awesome>.

94 <https://www.bing.com/search?q=awesome&form=STARH1&refig=a835ecff9dff4ec9a750fcb9df1726d3&mkt=en-us&ocid=&sp=1&qs=EP&pq=awesome&sc=10-7&cvid=a835ecff9dff4ec9a750fcb9df1726d3>.

95 Otto, *The Idea of the Holy*, 12–24.

96 Otto, *The Idea of the Holy*, 31–40.

97 Goodenough, *The Sacred Depths of Nature*, 9–15.

98 I have told this story also in "Conceptual Framework for a Curriculum in Social Change," *Journal of Social Change* 2018, 10, no. 1, (2018): 77. <https://doi.org/10.5590/JOSC.2018.10.1.06>

99 Eliade, *The Sacred and the Profane*, 11.

100 Eliade, *The Myth of the Eternal Return*, trans Willard R. Trask (Princeton, NJ: Princeton University Press, 1965), 317.

101 van Manen *Researching Lived Experience*, 101.
102 van Manen, *Researching Lived Experience*, 101–106. Van Manen also identifies corporeality as another existential (see endnote #70) and temporality (see endnote #139).
103 Eliade, *The Sacred and the Profane*, 12. See fn 86.
104 Tillich, *Ultimate Concern: Tillich in Dialogue*, 11. See fn 87.
105 Van der Merwe and Habron, "A Conceptual Model of Spirituality in Music Education," 59–60.
106 Mircea Eliade, *Patterns in Comparative Religion*, trans. Rosemary Sheed (New York: Meridian Books, 1958), 377.
107 Eliade, *Patterns in Comparative Religion*, 376.
108 Eliade, *Patterns in Comparative Religion*, 382, 383.
109 Eliade, *Patterns in Comparative Religion*, 384.
110 Eliade, *Patterns in Comparative Religion*, 385.
111 Eliade, *Patterns in Comparative Religion*, 383.
112 See David J. Tacey, *Edge of the Sacred: Transformation in Australia* (Melbourne: HarperCollins Australia,1995) and *The Way of the Spirit: Nature, Myth, and Magic in Native American Life* (Time-Life Books, 1997).
113 *The Way of the Spirit* (Time-Life Books, 1997), 13–64.
114 I was fortunate to visit a Sami family in 2023 and listen as they pointed to the river, the trees, the grasses, and even the reindeer as elements of a sacred environment.
115 John Dewey, *School and Society* (Chicago, University of Chicago Press, 1899). See also, John Dewey, *Democracy and Education* (NY: The Free Press, 1916).
116 Charles Dickens, *Hard Times* (Minneapolis, Minnesota: Lerner Publishing Group, 1905 edition), 9.
117 Dickens, *Hard Times*, 54.
118 Dickens, *Hard Times*, 11.
119 Dickens, *Hard Times*, 15.
120 Randall Everett Allsup, Review of Jane Roland Martin, *School Was Our Life* in *Philosophy of Music Education Review* 29, no. 2 (Fall, 2021): 234.
121 Maria Montessori, *From Childhood to Adolescence*, 2nd ed. (NY: Schocken Books, 1973), xv.
122 Montessori, *The Montessori Method*, 17, 18.
123 Maria Montessori, *The Montessori Method*, 101.
124 Jane Roland Martin, *School was our Life: Remembering Progressive Education* (Bloomington, Indiana: Indiana University Press, (2018), 3.
125 Martin, *School was our Life*, 5.
126 Martin, *School was our Life*, 30–31.
127 Martin, *School was our Life*, 32–33.

128 Martin, *School was our Life*, 99.

129 <https://www.lrei.org/about/mission-and-progressive-principles>.

130 Martin, *School was our Life*, 2. Italics in the original. Martin bemoans the accounts of progressive education and the prevailing sense that they failed the learners and American society. Such accounts in her mind do not understand or represent what progressive education was really about. See Chapter 5 Buried Treasure, 110–139.

131 Martin, *School was our Life*, 53.

132 See Iris M. Yob, *For Profit and For Good: Walden University 1970–2020* (Cambridge, UK: Ethics International Press, 2022), xv–xxi. See also, Iris M. Yob, "Progressive Education at a Distance," in *Driving Innovation with For-Profit Adult Higher Education Online Institutions*, eds Hilda Glazer, David Stein, and Constance Wanstreet (Hershey, PA: IGI Global, 2022): 20–43. <https://doi.org/10.4018/978-1-7998-9098-0>.

133 Yob, *For Profit and For Good*, 1–49.

134 For a fuller account, see Walter Kaufmann, *Religions in Four Dimensions: Existential, Aesthetic, Historical, and Comparative* (New York, Religious Digest Press, 1976) and Margaret Miles, *Image as Insight: Visual Understanding in Western Christianity and Secular Culture* (Boston: Beacon Press, 1985).

135 See, for instance, Jonathan Kozol, *Savage Inequalities: Children in American Schools* (New York: Crown Publishers, 1991). This theme began with his *Death at an Early Age* (1967) and has culminated in his latest, *An End to Inequality: Breaking Down the Walls of Apartheid Education in America* (2024).

136 Claire Detels, "Soft Boundaries," Praeger ebooks, 1999. Available at <https://www.academia.edu/123813887/Soft_Boundaries>.

137 Montessori, *The Montessori Method*, trans Anne E, George (NY: Frederick A Stokes Co., 1912), 44–49.

138 Jane Roland Martin, *The Schoolhome: Rethinking Schools for Changing Families* (Cambridge, MA: Harvard University Press, 1992).

139 Nel Noddings, *Starting at Home* (Berkley and Los Angeles, CA: California University Press, 2002).

140 Albi Odendaal, "A Musical Home with Many Rooms: Boundaries and Belonging," in *Ritualised Belonging: Musicing and Spirituality in the South African Context*, June Boyce-Tillman, Liese van der Merwe, and Janelize Morelli, eds (Oxford: Peter Lang, 2021), 93–109.

141 Rudolf Otto, *The Idea of the Holy*, trans. John Harvey (London: Oxford University Press [1923], 1950), chapter IV.

142 Otto, *The Idea of the Holy*, chapter VI.

143 Diana Eck, *Encountering God: From Bozeman to Banaras* (Boston: Beacon Press, 1993), 76–79.

144 June Boyce-Tillman, "The Transformative Qualities of a Liminal Space Created by Musicking," *Philosophy of Music Education Review* 17, no. 2 (Fall, 2009): 189.

145 Boyce-Tillman, "The Transformative Qualities of a Liminal Space Created by Musicking," 189.

146 van Manen, *Researching Lived Experience*, 104. Van Manen also identifies corporeality as another existential (see endnote #70) and spatiality (see endnote #98).

147 Ecclesiastes 3: 1–8 (KJV).

148 Van der Merwe and Habron, "A Conceptual Model of Spirituality in Music Education,"60–63.

149 This is a theme represented also in *Bildung* thought. See for instance, the articles celebrating the work of Frede V. Nielsen in *Philosophy of Music Education Review* 22, no. 2 (Fall 2014).

150 Gary Eberle, *Sacred Time and the Search for Meaning* (Boston: Shambhala, 2003).

151 I am indebted to June Boyce-Tillman who offered a similar idea during a discussion at the conference, Critical Perspectives on Religion, Music, and Education, Helsinki, Finland, August 2014.

152 Mason Currey, ed., *Daily Rituals: How Artists Work*. (NY: Knopf Publishers, 2013).

153 See for instance, <http://www.huffingtonpost.com/sean-mccloud/nones-somes-and-the-combinativeness-of-american-religious-practices-_b_2784390.html>.

154 The invention of the first clock by Benedictine monks and its purpose and impact is described by Eberle, *Sacred Time and the Search for Meaning*, 99–103.

155 Mircea Eliade, *The Sacred and the Profane: The Nature of Religion*, trans Willard R. Trask (San Diego: Harcourt Brace Javanovich, 1959), 11.

156 Anna Della Subin, "How to Stop Time: A Meditation on Procrastination," *New York Times* Sunday Review, September 28, 2014.

157 See the extract from Catholic Online about Expeditus at <http://www.catholic.org/saints/saint.php?saint_id=347>.

158 Subin, "How to Stop Time," 1.

159 Israel Scheffler, *In Praise of the Cognitive Emotions and Other Essays in the Philosophy of Education* (New York: Routledge, 1991), 134–136.

160 Scheffler, *In Praise of the Cognitive Emotions*,136–137.

161 Estelle Jorgensen, *Music Education Sins Redeemed*, book manuscript in preparation, Chapter 1, "Sloth."

162 Maggie Berg and Barbara K. Seeber, *The Slow Professor: Challenging the Culture of Speed in the Academy* (Toronto, University of Toronto Press, 2016), 15.

163 Berg and Seeber, *The Slow Professor*, 17.
164 Berg and Seeber, *The Slow Professor*, 18.
165 Berg and Seeber, *The Slow Professor*, 44–46.
166 Paul Tillich, quoted in *Paul Tillich: On Art and Architecture*, ed John Dillenger and Jane Dillenger (NY: Crossroad, 1989), xix.
167 See for example, Susanne K. Langer's trilogy, *Mind: An Essay on Human Feeling*, Vols. I–III (Baltimore: John Hopkins University Press, 1967, 1972, 1982); *Feeling and Form: A Theory of Art* (London: Routledge and Kegan Paul Ltd, 1953).
168 Mihaly Csikszentmihlyi, in *Flow: The Psychology of Optimal Experience (Steps Toward Enhancing the Quality of Life)* (NY: HarperCollins, 1990), describes this experience and its value.
169 Eliade, *Myth of the Eternal Return*, xv.
170 Eliade, *Myth of the Eternal Return*, 141.
171 Eliade, *Myth of the Eternal Return*, 151.
172 Eliade, *Myth of the Eternal Return*, 146.
173 Eliade, *Myth of the Eternal Return*, 147, 148
174 Eliade, *Myth of the Eternal Return*, 147–154.
175 For a fuller account of Eliade's conception of the role of the arts in understanding the sacred, see the selected collection of his writings, *Mircea Eliade, Symbolism, the Sacred, and the Arts*, ed. Diane Apostolos-Cappadona (NY: Crossroad, 1986).
176 Apostolos-Cappadona, *Mircea Eliade*, 53.
177 Eliade, *The Sacred and the Profane*, 75.
178 Eliade, *The Sacred and the Profane*, 201.
179 Even eschatological conceptions of time which point to a single future second coming and a final new earth have a significant problem, Eliade proclaims, because they fortify notions of historical time. See Eliade, *The Myth of the Eternal Return*, 60.
180 Israel Scheffler, *Inquiries: Philosophical Studies of Language, Science, ad Learning* (Indianapolis, IN: Hackett Publishing Co., 1986), 52–67.
181 See for instance, Mircea Eliade, *The Myth of the Eternal Return; or Cosmos and History*, trans Willard R. Trask (New Jersey: Princeton University Press, 1954); Mircea Eliade, *Myths, Dreams, and Mysteries*, trans. Philip Mairet (New York: Harper and Row, 1960).
182 Harvey Cox, *The Feast of Fools: A Theological Essay on Festivity and Fantasy* (New York: Harper and Row, 1969), 83–84.
183 For the original peoples of Australia, the re-enactment was not a celebration but a repeat and reminder of repression and oppression. The aboriginal peoples have created a new flag which is often seen flying side by side with the

national flag and functioning for them in a similar way. It is divided in two with a black top half representing the Aboriginal people of Australia; a red bottom half representing the red earth, the red ochre used in ceremonies, and Aboriginal peoples' spiritual relation to the land as well as representing the blood of the Aboriginal people; and a yellow circle in the middle, representing the sun, the giver and protector of life. See <https://en.wikipedia.org/wiki/Australian_Aboriginal_flag>.

184 Randall Collins, *Interaction Ritual Chains* (NJ: Princeton University Press, 2004).

185 Collins, *Interaction Ritual Chains*, 110.

186 In the collection, *Ritualised Belonging*, writers apply Collins framework of ingredients and outcomes to analyze classroom practices and propose ways teachers can effectively bring cohesion, energy, and focus to learning when there is so much to distract and detach us from each other in our "highly unequal and divided society." (5).

187 Collins, *Interaction Ritual Chains*, 121–142.

188 Collins, *Interaction Ritual Chains*, 116–120.

189 Collins, *Interaction Ritual Chains*, 34–37.

190 Shona Simkin, *Harvard Gazette*, Jan 23, 2023. <https://www.hbs.edu/news/articles/Pages/rituals-teaching.aspx?utm_source=SilverpopMailing&utm_medium=email&utm_campaign+Daily%20Gazette%2020230215%20(1)>.

191 *Pianoforte*, directed by Jakub Piątek; produced by Maciej Kubicki; written by Jakub Piątek, (2023) in Polish.

192 Eleni N. Gage, "The Power of Rituals," *Connections* (Nov 2020): 88–89.

193 Walden University bears a familiar name, but why was that name chosen, especially since the well-known Walden Pond is located in a different state from those ever occupied by the university? In researching the university's history, I found it is a question asked now by too few faculty members, administrators, investors, and students and yet the meaning, although nuanced, is rich with implication. The name was inspired by the writings of Henry David Thoreau, who was steeped in the romantic thought of the Transcendentalists and took residence for a time in a rough-hewn hut on the bank of Walden Pond in Massachusetts in order to reflect free from the distractions of communal life. Guidance, inspiration, and a level of confidence in what the university and its constituents have hoped to achieve through the years are captured in significant quotations from Thoreau's reflections, *Walden*, scattered through the early catalogs and publications of the university. Captured in the name of the university, Walden is a both a powerful vision and guidance for succeeding generations.

194 Émile Durkheim, *The Elementary Forms of Religious Life*, trans Joseph Ward Swain (New York: The Free Press, 1965), 388–390.

195 Richard Trumpbour, "The Role of Communication in the History of Stadium Construction," *Journal of Communication Inquiry* 31, no. 4 (Oct 2007): 311–313.

196 For the role of media as creators of ritual see Simon Cottle, "Mediatized Rituals: Beyond Manufacturing Consent," *Media, Culture, and Society* 28, no 3 (2006): 411–432.

197 Trumpbour, "The Role of Communication in the History of Stadium Construction."

198 Sara Malaquias, Carla Crespo, and Rita Francisco, "How do Adolescents Benefit from Family Rituals: Links to Social Connectedness, Depression and Anxiety," *Journal of Child and Family Studies* 24 (2015): 3009–3017.

199 In the collection, *Ritualised Belonging*, are accounts of music education that have recognized and entailed significant elements of ritualized experiences. For instance, Boudina McConnachie, "Social Cohesion through Sonic Intervention," 161–177; Urvi Drummond, "Authentic Connection through Emotional Experiences in Piano Lessons: A Piano Teacher's Autoethnographic Account of Care," 195–210; and Marelize van Herden, "Dance Education as an Agent of Social Cohesion, 249–267.

200 Cox, *The Feast of Fools*, 84–89.

201 Cottle, "Mediatized Rituals," 415.

202 Joel Robbins, "Ritual Pluralism and Value Pluralism: On Why One Ritual is Never Enough," *Suomen Antropologi* 41, no 4 (Winter 2016): 6–13.

203 See, e.g., <https://arstechnica.com/science/2023/03/gun-violence-is-the-top-killer-of-us-kids-the-pandemic-made-it-worse/>.

204 According to the Centers for Disease Control, in the United States, one in three girls were reported as having considered taking their own lives and more than half of being continually sad or suicidal and one in five students identifying as LGBQ+ had made an attempt at suicide. <https://www.caller.com/story/news/health/2023/03/20/mental-health-matters-teens-girls-at-record-high-levels-of-suicide-risk/70020161007/>.

205 June Boyce-Tillman, *Constructing Musical Healing: The Wounds that Sing* (London: Jessica Kingsley Publishers, 2000). See especially 128–168.

206 Starhawk, "Creating Community Ritual," *Communities*, no. 154 (Spring 2012): 12–14.

207 Boyce Tillman does not hesitate to use "transcend" in the context of healing rituals. See *Constructing Musical Healing*, 244.

208 The "ultimate" and "really real" are proposed by Paul Tillich and Mircea Eliade respectively as the goal for sacred understanding. These ideas are discussed in Chapter 3.

209 Chris van Rhyn, "*Because I could not stop for death*: Composing an Electronic Work as a Mourning and Healing Ritual," in *Ritualised Belonging*, 325–348.

210 June Boyce-Tillman, "Postlude: Musical Rituals for Reconciliation," in *Ritualised Belonging*, 167–376.

211 See Lorena Parrish, "Dismantling Domination through Womanist Rituals of Resistance," *Liturgy* 35 no. 1 (2020): 10–18. <https://www.tandfonline.com/doi/full/10.1080/0458063X.2020.1701897>.

212 Hanna M. Nikkanen and Heidi Westerlund, "More Than Just Music: Reconsidering the Educational Value of Music in School Rituals," *Philosophy of Music Education Review* 25, no. 2 (Fall, 2017): 121

213 Nikkanen and Westerlund, "More Than Just Music," 121.

214 Jay Johnson, "Through the Liminal: A Comparative Analysis of Communitas and Rites of Passage in Sport Hazing and Initiations," *Canadian Journal of Sociology*, 36, no. 3 (2011): 199–227; Diana Dias and Maria Jose Sa, "Transition to Higher Education: The Role of Initiation Practices," *Educational Research* 56, no. 1 (2014): 1–12.

215 In fact, New College had one of the largest intakes of international students in the US before being aligned with conservative values.

216 American Association of University Professors in "Report of a Special Committee: Political Interference and Academic Freedom in Florida's Public Higher Education System" gives a full description of events at New College from the perspective of professors. A typical newspaper report also outlines events at New College from January 2023 to early February, 2024: see, "A Tumultuos Transition: Conservative Makeover has Transformed Campus," *Sarasota Herald Times*, Feb 18, 2024, 1, 15A.

217 The former chair of the New College board of trustees, working with Bard College, arranged for accredited online courses for New College students that they no longer had access to through their onsite courses. The first offerings included a course offered by David Hogg, a survivor of the Parkland school shooting who had become a well-known advocate for gun control; a second course, offered by Masha Gessen and Judith Butler, was a study of authoritarianism.

218 I am grateful to Graça Mota for sharing and translating this from *Public*, December 11, 2024.

219 See Collins, *Interaction Ritual Chains* for further discussion in previous chapter.

220 See for example, David Palfreyman, "Is Academic Freedom under Threat in U.K. and U.S. Higher Education?" *Education and the Law*, 19, no. 1 (March 2007): 19–40; Susan L. Robertson and Matias Nestore, "Education Cleavages,

or Market Society and the Rise of Authoritarian Populism?" in *Globalisation, Societies and Education*, vol. 20, no. 2 (2022): 110–123 <https://doi.org/10.1080/14767724.2021.1955662>.

221 "Cancel culture" or "shaming" in this context is ignoring or denying the rights, values, or even existence of different others.

222 As reported in the *Sarasota Herald-Tribune USA TODAY NETWORK*, November 16, 2024.

223 A term suggested by Estelle Jorgensen where partisan groups are informed within their own bubble of influencers, often created in the digital world by social media in its various forms.

224 These criteria reflect Collins' four ingredients for interactive rituals. See fn #180.

225 Øivind Varkøy and Petter Dyndahl, "Do We All have to be 'Leftists:' A Dialogue about Antagonism and Agonism in Music Education Research," *Nordic Research in Music Education* 3 (2021): 2.

226 Lauren Kapalka Richerme, "Uses and Abuses of Gatekeeping: A Call for Affect, Ethics, and Rigor," *Philosophy of Music Education Review*, 33, no.1 (2025), 22–36. DOI: https://doi.org/10.2979/pme.00020.

227 Varkøy and Dyndahl, "Do We All have to be 'Leftists," 3, 4.

228 For a definition and explanation of the paradox of tolerance see, for example, <https://philosophyterms.com/paradox-of-tolerance/>.

229 Varkøy and Dyndahl, "Do We All have to be 'Leftists,"13–17.

230 Hanne Rinholm and Øivind Varkøy, "A Reflection on Philosophy of Music Education Scholarship: Publications, Internationalization, Gatekeeping, and 'Gap-Keeping,'" *Philosophy of Music Education Review*, 33, no. 1 (2025), 74–90. DOI: https://doi.org/10.2979/pme.00023.

231 Martin, *School Was Our Home*, 105–109.

232 For one view, see for example, Paul D. Miller, "What is Christian Nationalism?" <https://www.christianitytoday.com/2021/02/what-is-christian-nationalism/>.

233 Eliade, *Patterns in Comparative Religion*, 369.

234 See the opening to Chapter 1, p. 1.

235 See p. 74.

236 See pp. 70–72.

237 See p. 70.

238 See "Rituals for Community Building," pp. 108–112.

239 See pp. 101–02.

240 See "Awe," pp. 57–61.

241 See p. 108.

242 See pp. 139–140.

243 See "Asking the Right Questions," pp. 127–131.
244 See "Surprise," pp. 61–63.
245 See p. 26.
246 See "Inner Sancta," p. 82.
247 See "Rituals for Community Building," pp. 111–112.
248 See "Rituals for Change," pp. 115–116.

Index

Music and Spirituality

Edited by

JUNE BOYCE-TILLMAN

Music and Spirituality explores the relationships between spirituality and music in a variety of traditions and contexts including those in which human beings have performed music with spiritual intention or effect. It will address the plurality of modern society in the areas of musical style and philosophical and religious beliefs, and give respect to different positions regarding the place of music both in worship and in the wider society. It will include historical, anthropological, musicological, ethnomusicological, theological and philosophical dimensions and encourage multi- disciplinary and cross-disciplinary contributions.

It looks for well-researched studies with new and open approaches to spirituality and music and will encourage interesting innovative case-studies. Books within the series are subject to peer review and will include single and co-authored monographs as well as edited collections including conference proceedings. It will consider the use of musical material in either written or recorded form as part of submissions.

The Series Editor

The Rev. Professor June Boyce-Tillman MBE is Professor Emerita of Applied Music at the University of Winchester, where she ran the Centre for the Arts as Wellbeing and the Tavener centre for Music and Spirituality. She has wide experience in education, spirituality and music and has published widely in these areas. She is an Extraordinary Professor at North West University, South Africa. She is a self-supporting ordained Anglican Priest and received an MBE for her contribution to music and education.

Proposal submissions should be sent to oxford@peterlang.com

Vol. 1 June Boyce-Tillman
In Tune With Heaven Or Not: Women in Christian Liturgical Music. 2014. ISBN 978-3-0343-1777-1

Vol. 2 June Boyce-Tillman
Experiencing Music – Restoring the Spiritual: Music as Wellbeing. 2016. ISBN 978-3-0343-1952-2

Vol. 3 Sarah Morgan and June Boyce-Tillman
A River Rather Than a Road: The Community Choir as Spiritual Experience. 2016. ISBN 978-3-0343-2265-2

Vol. 4 Nancy L. Graham
They Bear Acquaintance: African American Spirituals and the Camp Meetings. 2016. ISBN 978-3-0343-2211-9

Vol. 5 June Boyce-Tillman (ed.)
Spirituality and Music Education: Perspectives from Three Continents. 2017. ISBN 978-1-78707-416-3

Vol. 6 June Boyce-Tillman
Freedom Song: Faith, Abuse, Music and Spirituality: A Lived Experience of Celebration. 2018. ISBN 978-1-78874-219-1

Vol. 7 Karin S. Hendricks and June Boyce-Tillman (eds)
Queering Freedom: Music, Identity, and Spirituality (Anthology from North America, UK and South Africa.) 2018. ISBN 978-1-78874-508-6

Vol. 8 Lynn Whidden and Paul Shore
Environment Matters: Why Song Sounds The Way It Does. 2019. ISBN 978-1-78874-493-5

Vol. 9 June Boyce-Tillman
Enlivening Faith: Music, Spirituality and Christian Theology. 2019. ISBN 978-1-78874-620-5

Vol. 10 Solveig McIntosh
Rivers of Sacred Sound: Chant. 2019. ISBN 978-1-78874-439-3

Vol. 11 June Boyce-Tillman and Anne-Marie Forbes
Heart's Ease: Spirituality in the Music of John Tavener. 2020. ISBN 978-1-78874-748-6

Vol. 12 Olugbenga Olusola Elijah Taiwo
The Return Beat - Interfacing with our Interface. 2021. ISBN 978-1-78707-939-7

Vol. 13 Karin S. Hendricks and June Boyce-Tillman (eds)
Authentic Connection: Music, Spirituality and Wellbeing. 2021. ISBN 978-1-80079-159-6

Vol. 14 June Boyce-Tillman and Karin S. Hendricks (eds)
Living Song: Singing, Spirituality, and Wellbeing. 2021. ISBN 978-1-80079-075-9

Vol. 15 June Boyce-Tillman, Liesl van der Merwe and Janelize Morelli (eds)
Ritualised Belonging: Musicing and Spirituality in the South African Context. 2021. ISBN 978-1-80079-584-6

Vol. 16 Jillian Schofield and June Boyce-Tillman
A Rhythm for Wellbeing: A Therapist Reflects. 2024. ISBN 978-1-80079-917-2

Vol. 17 Iris M. Yob
School is Sacred: A Philosophy of Education for Our Time. 2026. ISBN 978-1-80374-685-2

www.ingramcontent.com/pod-product-compliance
Ingram Content Group UK Ltd.
Pitfield, Milton Keynes, MK11 3LW, UK
UKHW020159290926
15471UKWH00005B/963

9 781803 746852